# 105 Weight Control Recipe for Home

By: Kelly Johnson

**Table of Contents**

Recipes

Breakfast:

- Quinoa Breakfast Bowl with Fresh Berries
- Veggie Omelette with Spinach and Tomatoes
- Greek Yogurt Parfait with Nuts and Honey
- Whole Grain Pancakes with Blueberry Compote
- Avocado Toast with Poached Egg
- Chia Seed Pudding with Almond Milk
- Banana Walnut Smoothie
- Sweet Potato and Black Bean Breakfast Burrito
- Cottage Cheese and Pineapple Bowl
- Smoked Salmon and Cheese Bagel

Lunch:

- Grilled Chicken Salad with Mixed Greens
- Quinoa and Black Bean Stuffed Peppers
- Turkey and Avocado Wrap
- Lentil Soup with Vegetables
- Asian-Inspired Tofu Stir-Fry
- Cauliflower Fried Rice
- Chickpea and Veggie Buddha Bowl
- Spinach and Feta Turkey Burger
- Zucchini Noodles with Pesto

- Greek Salad with Grilled Shrimp

Dinner:

- Baked Salmon with Lemon and Dill
- Spaghetti Squash with Tomato Sauce
- Grilled Chicken Breast with Quinoa Pilaf
- Roasted Brussels Sprouts and Sweet Potatoes
- Shrimp and Broccoli Stir-Fry
- Stuffed Portobello Mushrooms with Quinoa
- Turkey Chili with Black Beans
- Eggplant Parmesan with Whole Wheat Pasta
- Grilled Veggie Skewers with Tofu
- Cod Fish Tacos with Cabbage Slaw

Snacks:

- Hummus and Veggie Sticks
- Greek Yogurt with Berries
- Air-Popped Popcorn with Nutritional Yeast
- Apple Slices with Almond Butter
- Edamame with Sea Salt
- Cottage Cheese with Pineapple
- Trail Mix with Nuts and Dried Fruit
- Roasted Chickpeas with Paprika
- Cucumber Slices with Tzatziki
- Hard-Boiled Eggs with Mustard

Soups:

- Butternut Squash Soup
- Minestrone Soup with Whole Wheat Pasta
- Chicken and Vegetable Soup
- Gazpacho with Cucumber and Tomatoes
- Quinoa and Kale Soup
- Black Bean Soup with Lime
- Tomato Basil Soup with Chickpeas
- Miso Soup with Tofu and Seaweed
- Lentil and Spinach Soup
- Creamy Broccoli Soup with Greek Yogurt

Salads:

- Kale and Quinoa Salad with Cranberries
- Caprese Salad with Balsamic Glaze
- Watermelon and Feta Salad
- Roasted Beet Salad with Goat Cheese
- Caesar Salad with Grilled Chicken
- Mango Avocado Salad with Lime Dressing
- Asian Cabbage Salad with Sesame Ginger Dressing
- Greek Salad with Quinoa
- Spinach and Strawberry Salad
- Tuna Salad Lettuce Wraps

Vegetarian:

- Lentil and Vegetable Stir-Fry
- Stuffed Bell Peppers with Quinoa and Black Beans
- Eggplant and Chickpea Curry
- Portobello Mushroom Burger
- Sweet Potato and Black Bean Enchiladas
- Spinach and Feta Stuffed Mushrooms
- Cauliflower Pizza Crust with Veggie Toppings
- Zucchini and Tomato Gratin
- Quinoa and Black Bean Quesadillas
- Broccoli and Cheddar Stuffed Potatoes

Chicken Dishes:

- Baked Lemon Garlic Chicken
- Chicken and Vegetable Skewers
- Grilled Chicken Caesar Salad
- Cilantro Lime Chicken with Quinoa
- Teriyaki Chicken Stir-Fry
- Pesto Chicken with Roasted Vegetables
- Chicken and Broccoli Casserole
- Honey Mustard Glazed Chicken Thighs
- Mediterranean Chicken with Olives and Tomatoes
- BBQ Chicken Lettuce Wraps

Seafood:

- Baked Cod with Herbs

- Shrimp and Vegetable Stir-Fry
- Lemon Garlic Butter Salmon
- Tuna and Avocado Salad
- Seared Scallops with Asparagus
- Grilled Mahi-Mahi with Mango Salsa
- Cajun Spiced Tilapia with Quinoa
- Crab and Avocado Stuffed Bell Peppers
- Spicy Sriracha Shrimp Lettuce Wraps
- Baked Halibut with Roasted Vegetables

Desserts:

- Greek Yogurt Parfait with Fresh Fruit
- Dark Chocolate-Dipped Strawberries
- Baked Apple with Cinnamon and Nutmeg
- Berry Sorbet with Mint
- Avocado Chocolate Mousse
- Chia Seed Pudding with Berries
- Frozen Banana Bites with Almond Butter
- Coconut and Mango Rice Pudding
- Pumpkin Spice Energy Bites
- Yogurt and Berry Popsicles

Beverages:

- Green Tea with Lemon and Mint
- Infused Water with Cucumber and Berries

- Matcha Latte with Almond Milk
- Berry Smoothie with Spinach
- Iced Herbal Tea with Citrus Slices

# Breakfast:

**Quinoa Breakfast Bowl with Fresh Berries:**

Ingredients:

- 1/2 cup quinoa (rinsed)
- 1 cup water
- 1 cup skim milk or a plant-based milk of your choice
- 1/2 teaspoon vanilla extract
- 1 tablespoon honey or maple syrup (optional, for sweetness)
- 1 cup mixed fresh berries (such as strawberries, blueberries, raspberries)
- 1 tablespoon chia seeds
- 1 tablespoon slivered almonds or chopped nuts
- Fresh mint leaves for garnish (optional)

Instructions:

Cook Quinoa:

- In a saucepan, combine quinoa and water.
- Bring to a boil, then reduce heat to low, cover, and simmer for about 15 minutes or until the quinoa is cooked and water is absorbed.
- Fluff the quinoa with a fork.

Prepare Quinoa Base:

- In a separate saucepan, heat the milk over medium heat. Add the cooked quinoa to the milk.
- Stir in vanilla extract and honey/maple syrup if using.

- Cook for an additional 5-7 minutes, stirring occasionally until the mixture thickens.

Assemble the Bowl:
- Divide the quinoa mixture into serving bowls.
- Top each bowl with a generous portion of mixed fresh berries.

Add Nutritional Boosters:
- Sprinkle chia seeds and slivered almonds over the berries.
- These ingredients add extra fiber, omega-3 fatty acids, and a satisfying crunch.

Garnish:
- Garnish with fresh mint leaves for a burst of freshness (optional).

Enjoy:
- Serve the quinoa breakfast bowl warm and enjoy a delicious and nutritious start to your day!

This breakfast bowl is not only flavorful but also packed with nutrients that can help keep you full and satisfied, making it a great choice for weight control. Adjust the sweetness and toppings according to your preferences and dietary needs.

**Veggie Omelette with Spinach and Tomatoes:**

Ingredients:

- 2 large eggs
- 1 cup fresh spinach, chopped
- 1/2 cup cherry tomatoes, halved
- 1/4 cup diced onions
- 1/4 cup bell peppers (any color), diced
- 1 clove garlic, minced
- 1 tablespoon olive oil or cooking spray
- Salt and pepper to taste
- Fresh herbs (such as parsley or chives) for garnish (optional)

Instructions:

Prepare Vegetables:

- Heat olive oil in a non-stick skillet over medium heat.
- Add diced onions and cook until translucent.
- Add minced garlic and cook for an additional 30 seconds.
- Add diced bell peppers and cook for 2-3 minutes until slightly softened.
- Add chopped spinach and cook until wilted.

Add Tomatoes:

- Add halved cherry tomatoes to the skillet and cook for an additional 1-2 minutes until they are heated through but still firm.

Whisk Eggs:

- In a bowl, whisk the eggs until well beaten.

- Season with salt and pepper to taste.

Cook Omelette:

- Pour the beaten eggs over the cooked vegetables in the skillet.
- Allow the eggs to set around the edges. Gently lift the edges with a spatula to let uncooked eggs flow underneath.

Fold and Serve:

- Once the eggs are mostly set, carefully fold the omelette in half with the spatula.
- Cook for an additional 1-2 minutes until the eggs are fully cooked and the vegetables are evenly distributed.

Garnish and Enjoy:

- Slide the omelette onto a plate and garnish with fresh herbs if desired.
- Serve hot and enjoy your nutritious veggie omelette!

This veggie omelette is a low-calorie, high-protein option that's perfect for a weight control plan. Feel free to customize the vegetables based on your preferences, and you can also add a sprinkle of cheese if desired (keeping in mind the calorie content).

**Veggie Omelette with Spinach and Tomatoes:**

Ingredients:

- 2 large eggs
- 1 cup fresh spinach, chopped
- 1/2 cup cherry tomatoes, halved
- 1/4 cup diced onions
- 1/4 cup bell peppers (any color), diced
- 1 clove garlic, minced
- 1 tablespoon olive oil or cooking spray
- Salt and pepper to taste
- Fresh herbs (such as parsley or chives) for garnish (optional)

Instructions:

Prepare Vegetables:

- Heat olive oil in a non-stick skillet over medium heat.
- Add diced onions and cook until translucent.
- Add minced garlic and cook for an additional 30 seconds.
- Add diced bell peppers and cook for 2-3 minutes until slightly softened.
- Add chopped spinach and cook until wilted.

Add Tomatoes:

- Add halved cherry tomatoes to the skillet and cook for an additional 1-2 minutes until they are heated through but still firm.

Whisk Eggs:

- In a bowl, whisk the eggs until well beaten.

- Season with salt and pepper to taste.

Cook Omelette:

- Pour the beaten eggs over the cooked vegetables in the skillet.
- Allow the eggs to set around the edges. Gently lift the edges with a spatula to let uncooked eggs flow underneath.

Fold and Serve:

- Once the eggs are mostly set, carefully fold the omelette in half with the spatula.
- Cook for an additional 1-2 minutes until the eggs are fully cooked and the vegetables are evenly distributed.

Garnish and Enjoy:

- Slide the omelette onto a plate and garnish with fresh herbs if desired.
- Serve hot and enjoy your nutritious veggie omelette!

This veggie omelette is a low-calorie, high-protein option that's perfect for a weight control plan. Feel free to customize the vegetables based on your preferences, and you can also add a sprinkle of cheese if desired (keeping in mind the calorie content).

**Greek Yogurt Parfait with Nuts and Honey:**

Ingredients:

- 1 cup non-fat Greek yogurt
- 1/4 cup mixed nuts (such as almonds, walnuts, or pistachios), chopped
- 1 tablespoon honey
- 1/2 cup mixed berries (such as blueberries, strawberries, raspberries)
- 1 tablespoon chia seeds (optional)
- 1 tablespoon shredded coconut (optional)
- Fresh mint leaves for garnish (optional)

Instructions:

Prepare Greek Yogurt:

- Spoon the Greek yogurt into a serving bowl or glass.

Add Mixed Nuts:

- Sprinkle the chopped mixed nuts over the Greek yogurt.
- Nuts provide healthy fats and a satisfying crunch.

Drizzle with Honey:

- Drizzle honey over the yogurt and nuts. Adjust the amount according to your sweetness preference.

Layer with Berries:

- Add a layer of mixed berries on top of the nuts and honey.
- Berries are rich in antioxidants and add natural sweetness.

Optional Additions:

- Sprinkle chia seeds and shredded coconut over the berries for added fiber and texture.

Garnish and Serve:

- Garnish with fresh mint leaves if desired.

Enjoy:

- Dive into your delicious and nutritious Greek yogurt parfait with nuts and honey!

This parfait is a balanced and satisfying snack or breakfast option. The Greek yogurt provides protein, while nuts contribute healthy fats. The berries add natural sweetness and a boost of antioxidants. Adjust the portions based on your dietary needs and preferences, and feel free to experiment with different nut and berry combinations.

**Whole Grain Pancakes with Blueberry Compote:**

Ingredients:

For the Whole Grain Pancakes:

- 1 cup whole grain flour
- 1 tablespoon baking powder
- 1 tablespoon honey or maple syrup
- 1 cup skim milk or a plant-based milk alternative
- 1 large egg
- 2 tablespoons melted coconut oil or unsweetened applesauce
- 1 teaspoon vanilla extract
- Pinch of salt

For the Blueberry Compote:

- 1 cup fresh or frozen blueberries
- 1 tablespoon honey or maple syrup
- 1 tablespoon lemon juice
- 1 teaspoon cornstarch mixed with 1 tablespoon water (optional, for thickening)

Instructions:

For the Whole Grain Pancakes:

- Prepare Dry Ingredients:
  - In a large bowl, whisk together the whole grain flour, baking powder, and a pinch of salt.

Combine Wet Ingredients:

- In a separate bowl, whisk together the egg, honey or maple syrup, milk, melted coconut oil or applesauce, and vanilla extract.

Mix Batter:

- Pour the wet ingredients into the dry ingredients and stir until just combined. Do not overmix; it's okay if there are a few lumps.

Cook Pancakes:

- Heat a griddle or non-stick skillet over medium heat. Lightly grease with cooking spray or a small amount of oil.
- Pour 1/4 cup portions of batter onto the griddle to form pancakes. Cook until bubbles form on the surface, then flip and cook until both sides are golden brown.

For the Blueberry Compote:

Prepare Blueberry Compote:

- In a small saucepan, combine blueberries, honey or maple syrup, and lemon juice.
- Cook over medium heat, stirring occasionally, until the blueberries break down and the mixture thickens slightly.
- If desired, mix cornstarch with water and add it to the compote to thicken further. Stir well.

Serve:

- Stack the whole grain pancakes on a plate and top with the blueberry compote.

Enjoy:

- Enjoy your delicious and nutritious whole grain pancakes with blueberry compote as a tasty and satisfying breakfast option!

This recipe provides a good balance of whole grains, fiber, and natural sweetness from the blueberries. Adjust the sweetness according to your taste preferences, and feel free to add a dollop of Greek yogurt or a sprinkle of chopped nuts for extra protein and texture.

**Avocado Toast with Poached Egg:**

Ingredients:

- 1 slice whole grain bread (or your preferred bread)
- 1/2 ripe avocado
- 1 large egg
- Salt and pepper to taste
- Red pepper flakes (optional, for added spice)
- Fresh herbs (such as parsley or chives) for garnish (optional)
- Lemon wedges for serving (optional)

Instructions:

Prepare Avocado:

- Mash the ripe avocado in a bowl using a fork.
- Season the mashed avocado with salt and pepper to taste. Optionally, add a dash of red pepper flakes for some heat.

Toast the Bread:

- Toast the slice of whole grain bread to your liking.

Spread Avocado:

- Spread the mashed avocado evenly over the toasted bread.

Poach the Egg:

- Poach the egg using your preferred method. One common method is to bring a pot of water to a simmer, add a splash of vinegar, and gently slide the egg into the simmering water. Cook until the whites are set but the yolk is still runny, about 3-4 minutes.

Assemble:
- Carefully place the poached egg on top of the avocado-covered toast.

Season and Garnish:
- Sprinkle the poached egg with a bit of salt and pepper.
- Garnish with fresh herbs if desired.

Serve:
- Serve the avocado toast with poached egg immediately.

Optional:
- Squeeze a bit of fresh lemon juice over the top for extra flavor.

Enjoy:
- Enjoy your delicious and satisfying avocado toast with poached egg!

This meal is rich in healthy fats, fiber, and protein, making it a filling and nutritious option. The whole grain bread adds complex carbohydrates, contributing to the overall balance of the meal. Adjust the portion sizes based on your dietary needs and preferences.

**Chia Seed Pudding with Almond Milk:**

Ingredients:

- 1/4 cup chia seeds
- 1 cup unsweetened almond milk
- 1/2 teaspoon vanilla extract
- 1 tablespoon maple syrup or honey (optional, for sweetness)
- Fresh fruits, berries, or nuts for topping (optional)

Instructions:

Mix Chia Seeds and Almond Milk:
- In a bowl or jar, combine chia seeds, almond milk, and vanilla extract. Stir well to ensure the chia seeds are evenly distributed.

Sweeten (Optional):
- If desired, add maple syrup or honey to sweeten the mixture. Adjust the sweetness according to your taste preferences.

Stir and Refrigerate:
- Stir the mixture again after a few minutes to prevent clumping, then cover and refrigerate for at least 2 hours or overnight. The chia seeds will absorb the liquid and create a pudding-like consistency.

Check and Stir:
- After the initial refrigeration period, check the pudding's consistency. If it's too thick, you can add a bit more almond milk and stir until well combined.

Serve:
- Spoon the chia seed pudding into serving bowls or jars.

Top with Fresh Fruits or Nuts (Optional):

- Add your favorite toppings, such as fresh fruits, berries, or nuts, for added flavor, texture, and nutritional value.

Enjoy:

- Enjoy your chia seed pudding with almond milk as a nutritious and satisfying snack or breakfast option!

This chia seed pudding is a great source of fiber, healthy fats, and plant-based protein. It's customizable, so feel free to experiment with different flavors, toppings, or sweeteners based on your preferences. Additionally, it's a good idea to portion control, especially if you are following a weight control plan.

**Banana Walnut Smoothie:**

Ingredients:

- 1 ripe banana
- 1/4 cup walnuts
- 1 cup unsweetened almond milk (or any other milk of your choice)
- 1/2 cup Greek yogurt (plain, non-fat)
- 1 tablespoon chia seeds (optional, for added fiber)
- Ice cubes (optional)
- Honey or maple syrup (optional, for added sweetness)

Instructions:

Prepare Ingredients:
- Peel the ripe banana and break it into chunks.
- If the walnuts are not already chopped, roughly chop them.

Blend:
- In a blender, combine the banana chunks, chopped walnuts, almond milk, Greek yogurt, and chia seeds.

Blend Until Smooth:
- Blend the ingredients until smooth and creamy. If the smoothie is too thick, you can add more almond milk to reach your desired consistency.

Sweeten (Optional):
- If you prefer a sweeter taste, you can add a drizzle of honey or maple syrup. Keep in mind that the ripe banana already adds natural sweetness.

Add Ice Cubes (Optional):

- If you like a colder smoothie, you can add a handful of ice cubes and blend again until well incorporated.

Pour and Serve:

- Pour the smoothie into a glass.

Garnish (Optional):

- Garnish with a few additional chopped walnuts on top for added texture.

Enjoy:

- Enjoy your Banana Walnut Smoothie as a nutritious and filling snack or breakfast option!

This smoothie provides a good balance of carbohydrates, healthy fats, and protein, making it a satisfying option. It's important to be mindful of portion sizes, especially if you are managing your calorie intake for weight control. Adjust the ingredients and sweetness according to your taste preferences and dietary needs.

**Sweet Potato and Black Bean Breakfast Burrito:**

Ingredients:

- 1 medium-sized sweet potato, peeled and diced
- 1/2 cup black beans, cooked and drained
- 2 large eggs
- 1 teaspoon olive oil
- 1/4 teaspoon cumin
- 1/4 teaspoon paprika
- Salt and pepper to taste
- Whole-grain or spinach tortillas
- Salsa or hot sauce for serving
- Fresh cilantro, chopped (optional, for garnish)

Instructions:

Cook Sweet Potato:
- In a skillet, heat olive oil over medium heat. Add the diced sweet potato and cook until tender, about 8-10 minutes.

Add Black Beans:
- Add the black beans to the skillet with the sweet potato. Stir to combine and heat through.

Season:
- Sprinkle cumin, paprika, salt, and pepper over the sweet potato and black bean mixture. Stir to evenly coat the ingredients with the spices.

Scramble Eggs:

- Push the sweet potato and black bean mixture to one side of the skillet. Crack the eggs into the other side and scramble them until cooked through.

Combine:
- Once the eggs are cooked, mix them in with the sweet potato and black bean mixture. Ensure that the spices are evenly distributed.

Warm Tortillas:
- Warm the tortillas in a dry skillet or microwave according to package instructions.

Assemble Burritos:
- Place a portion of the sweet potato, black bean, and egg mixture in the center of each tortilla.

Fold and Roll:
- Fold the sides of the tortilla in, then fold the bottom up and roll to form a burrito.

Serve:
- Place the burritos seam-side down on the skillet to seal, then remove and serve.

Garnish and Enjoy:
- Serve the burritos with salsa or hot sauce, and garnish with fresh cilantro if desired.

This Sweet Potato and Black Bean Breakfast Burrito is a balanced meal, providing complex carbohydrates, protein, and healthy fats. Adjust the portion sizes based on your dietary needs and preferences. It can be a filling breakfast or brunch option that supports your weight control goals.

**Cottage Cheese and Pineapple Bowl:**

Ingredients:

- 1 cup low-fat cottage cheese
- 1 cup fresh pineapple chunks (or canned pineapple in juice, drained)
- 1 tablespoon honey (optional, for added sweetness)
- 1 tablespoon chopped nuts (such as almonds or walnuts, optional)
- Fresh mint leaves for garnish (optional)

Instructions:

Prepare Cottage Cheese:
- Scoop the cottage cheese into a serving bowl.

Add Pineapple Chunks:
- Add the fresh pineapple chunks on top of the cottage cheese.

Sweeten (Optional):
- If you desire extra sweetness, drizzle honey over the cottage cheese and pineapple. Adjust the amount based on your preference.

Top with Nuts (Optional):
- Sprinkle chopped nuts over the mixture for added crunch and healthy fats.

Garnish:
- Garnish the bowl with fresh mint leaves for a burst of freshness and color.

Serve:
- Serve the Cottage Cheese and Pineapple Bowl immediately.

Enjoy:
- Enjoy this simple and nutritious snack or light meal!

This combination is rich in protein, vitamins, and minerals. It provides a good balance of macronutrients and can be a satisfying option for those looking to manage their weight. Feel free to customize the toppings based on your preferences, adding other fruits, seeds, or a sprinkle of cinnamon for additional flavor. Adjust the portion sizes according to your dietary needs.

**Smoked Salmon and Cheese Bagel:**

Ingredients:

- 1 whole grain or multigrain bagel (sliced and toasted)
- 2-3 ounces smoked salmon
- 2 tablespoons cream cheese (reduced-fat or light)
- 1 tablespoon capers (optional, for added flavor)
- Sliced red onion (optional, for added crunch and flavor)
- Fresh dill for garnish (optional)
- Lemon wedges for serving

Instructions:

Prepare Bagel:
- Slice the whole grain or multigrain bagel and toast it to your liking.

Spread Cream Cheese:
- Spread the cream cheese evenly on each half of the toasted bagel.

Layer Smoked Salmon:
- Lay the smoked salmon over the cream cheese. Ensure it covers the bagel evenly.

Add Toppings:
- If using, sprinkle capers over the smoked salmon. Add sliced red onion for additional flavor and crunch.

Garnish:
- Garnish with fresh dill for a burst of herbaceous flavor.

Serve with Lemon Wedges:

- Serve the Smoked Salmon and Cheese Bagel with lemon wedges on the side. Squeezing fresh lemon juice over the salmon can enhance the flavors.

Enjoy:

- Enjoy your delicious and nutritious Smoked Salmon and Cheese Bagel!

This meal is rich in omega-3 fatty acids from the salmon, protein from both the salmon and cream cheese, and complex carbohydrates from the whole grain bagel. Adjust the portion sizes based on your dietary needs and preferences. It's a satisfying option for breakfast, brunch, or a light meal.

# Lunch:

## Grilled Chicken Salad with Mixed Greens:

Ingredients:

For the Salad:

- 6 ounces boneless, skinless chicken breast
- Salt and pepper to taste
- 6 cups mixed salad greens (such as spinach, arugula, and romaine)
- 1 cup cherry tomatoes, halved
- 1 cucumber, sliced
- 1 bell pepper, thinly sliced
- 1/4 red onion, thinly sliced
- 1/4 cup feta cheese, crumbled (optional)
- 1/4 cup Kalamata olives, pitted and halved (optional)

For the Grilled Chicken:

- 1 tablespoon olive oil
- 1 teaspoon dried oregano
- 1 teaspoon garlic powder
- Juice of 1 lemon

For the Dressing:

- 2 tablespoons extra-virgin olive oil
- 1 tablespoon balsamic vinegar

- 1 teaspoon Dijon mustard
- Salt and pepper to taste

Instructions:

For the Grilled Chicken:

Marinate Chicken:

- In a bowl, mix olive oil, dried oregano, garlic powder, and lemon juice. Season the chicken breast with salt and pepper, then coat it with the marinade. Let it marinate for at least 30 minutes.

Grill Chicken:

- Preheat the grill or a grill pan over medium-high heat. Grill the chicken for about 6-8 minutes per side or until fully cooked. Let it rest for a few minutes before slicing.

For the Salad:

Prepare Vegetables:

- In a large salad bowl, combine the mixed greens, cherry tomatoes, cucumber, bell pepper, red onion, feta cheese (if using), and Kalamata olives (if using).

For the Dressing:

Make Dressing:

- In a small bowl, whisk together the extra-virgin olive oil, balsamic vinegar, Dijon mustard, salt, and pepper.

Assemble the Salad:

- Slice Chicken:
    - Slice the grilled chicken into thin strips.
- Combine:
    - Add the sliced grilled chicken to the salad bowl with the mixed greens and vegetables.
- Drizzle Dressing:
    - Drizzle the dressing over the salad and toss gently to coat.
- Serve:
    - Divide the salad among serving plates or bowls.
- Enjoy:
    - Enjoy your Grilled Chicken Salad with Mixed Greens as a nutritious and satisfying meal for weight control!

This salad is not only full of flavor but also provides a good balance of protein, fiber, and healthy fats. Adjust the ingredient quantities and dressing according to your preferences and dietary needs.

**Quinoa and Black Bean Stuffed Peppers:**

Ingredients:

- 4 large bell peppers (any color)
- 1 cup quinoa, cooked
- 1 can (15 oz) black beans, drained and rinsed
- 1 cup corn kernels (fresh, frozen, or canned)
- 1 cup diced tomatoes (fresh or canned)
- 1/2 cup red onion, finely chopped
- 1 teaspoon cumin
- 1 teaspoon chili powder
- 1/2 teaspoon garlic powder
- Salt and pepper to taste
- 1 cup shredded cheese (cheddar, pepper jack, or your choice)
- Fresh cilantro or parsley for garnish (optional)
- Lime wedges for serving (optional)

Instructions:

Preheat Oven:

- Preheat the oven to 375°F (190°C).

Prepare Peppers:

- Cut the tops off the bell peppers, remove the seeds and membranes. Lightly brush the outside of the peppers with olive oil and place them in a baking dish.

Prepare Filling:

- In a large bowl, combine cooked quinoa, black beans, corn, diced tomatoes, red onion, cumin, chili powder, garlic powder, salt, and pepper. Mix well.

Stuff Peppers:

- Stuff each bell pepper with the quinoa and black bean mixture, pressing down gently to pack the filling.

Top with Cheese:

- Sprinkle shredded cheese over the top of each stuffed pepper.

Bake:

- Cover the baking dish with aluminum foil and bake in the preheated oven for about 25-30 minutes, or until the peppers are tender.

Broil (Optional):

- If you want a golden-brown cheesy top, you can uncover the peppers and broil for an additional 2-3 minutes.

Garnish and Serve:

- Garnish with fresh cilantro or parsley if desired. Serve the stuffed peppers with lime wedges on the side.

Enjoy:

- Enjoy your Quinoa and Black Bean Stuffed Peppers as a delicious and nutritious meal for weight control!

This dish is high in fiber, protein, and essential nutrients. It's a well-balanced option that can be a part of a healthy eating plan. Adjust the seasoning and cheese according to your taste preferences, and feel free to customize the recipe with additional vegetables or toppings.

**Turkey and Avocado Wrap:**

Ingredients:

- 1 whole wheat or spinach tortilla
- 4 ounces lean turkey breast, thinly sliced
- 1/2 avocado, sliced
- 1 cup mixed salad greens (spinach, arugula, or your choice)
- 1/4 cup cherry tomatoes, halved
- 1/4 cup cucumber, sliced
- 1 tablespoon plain Greek yogurt or light mayo
- 1 teaspoon Dijon mustard
- Salt and pepper to taste

Instructions:

Prepare Ingredients:
- Lay out the whole wheat or spinach tortilla on a flat surface.

Spread Greek Yogurt/Mayo and Mustard:
- In a small bowl, mix the Greek yogurt or light mayo with Dijon mustard. Spread this mixture evenly over the tortilla.

Layer Turkey:
- Place the thinly sliced turkey evenly over the spread.

Add Avocado Slices:
- Lay the avocado slices on top of the turkey.

Add Salad Greens, Tomatoes, and Cucumber:

- Place the mixed salad greens, halved cherry tomatoes, and sliced cucumber over the turkey and avocado.

Season:

- Season with salt and pepper to taste.

Wrap:

- Fold the sides of the tortilla in, then fold the bottom up, and roll to form a wrap.

Serve:

- Slice the wrap in half diagonally and serve.

Enjoy:

- Enjoy your Turkey and Avocado Wrap as a delicious and satisfying meal!

This wrap is a good source of protein, healthy fats, and fiber. It's versatile, and you can customize it by adding other veggies or a squeeze of lemon for extra flavor. Adjust the portion sizes based on your dietary needs and preferences. It's a convenient and tasty option for a quick lunch or dinner.

**Lentil Soup with Vegetables:**

Ingredients:

- 1 cup dried lentils (green or brown), rinsed and drained
- 1 onion, finely chopped
- 2 carrots, diced
- 2 celery stalks, diced
- 3 cloves garlic, minced
- 1 can (14 oz) diced tomatoes (with juice)
- 6 cups vegetable broth (low-sodium)
- 1 teaspoon ground cumin
- 1 teaspoon ground coriander
- 1/2 teaspoon smoked paprika
- Salt and pepper to taste
- 2 cups kale or spinach, chopped
- Juice of 1 lemon
- Olive oil for drizzling (optional)
- Fresh parsley for garnish (optional)

Instructions:

Prepare Lentils:

- Rinse and drain the lentils.

Sauté Vegetables:

- In a large pot, heat a bit of olive oil over medium heat. Add chopped onions, carrots, and celery. Sauté until the vegetables are softened, about 5 minutes.

Add Garlic and Spices:

- Add minced garlic, ground cumin, ground coriander, and smoked paprika. Stir and cook for an additional 1-2 minutes until fragrant.

Combine Lentils and Broth:

- Add the rinsed lentils, diced tomatoes (with juice), and vegetable broth to the pot. Season with salt and pepper to taste.

Simmer:

- Bring the soup to a boil, then reduce the heat to low. Cover and simmer for about 20-25 minutes or until the lentils are tender.

Add Greens and Lemon Juice:

- Stir in the chopped kale or spinach and cook until wilted. Add lemon juice to brighten the flavors.

Adjust Seasoning:

- Taste the soup and adjust the seasoning if necessary.

Serve:

- Ladle the lentil soup into bowls. Drizzle with a bit of olive oil (optional) and garnish with fresh parsley if desired.

Enjoy:

- Enjoy your delicious and wholesome Lentil Soup with Vegetables!

This soup is not only flavorful but also a great source of plant-based protein and fiber. It's filling and can be a satisfying part of a weight control plan. Adjust the vegetable quantities and seasonings based on your preferences.

**Asian-Inspired Tofu Stir-Fry:**

Ingredients:

For the Stir-Fry:

- 1 block extra-firm tofu, pressed and cubed
- 2 cups broccoli florets
- 1 bell pepper, thinly sliced
- 1 carrot, julienned
- 1 cup snap peas, ends trimmed
- 1 cup sliced mushrooms
- 3 green onions, chopped
- 2 tablespoons sesame oil (divided)
- 3 cloves garlic, minced
- 1 tablespoon ginger, grated
- 1/4 cup low-sodium soy sauce or tamari
- 1 tablespoon hoisin sauce
- 1 tablespoon rice vinegar
- 1 tablespoon maple syrup or honey
- Red pepper flakes (optional, for heat)
- Sesame seeds for garnish (optional)
- Cooked brown rice or quinoa for serving

Instructions:

Prepare Tofu:

- Press the tofu to remove excess water, then cut it into cubes.

Sauté Tofu:

- Heat 1 tablespoon of sesame oil in a large wok or skillet over medium-high heat. Add the tofu cubes and cook until they are golden brown on all sides. Remove tofu from the pan and set aside.

Stir-Fry Vegetables:

- In the same pan, add the remaining tablespoon of sesame oil. Add garlic and ginger, and sauté for about 30 seconds until fragrant.
- Add broccoli, bell pepper, carrot, snap peas, and mushrooms. Stir-fry the vegetables for 4-5 minutes until they are tender-crisp.

Combine Tofu and Sauce:

- Return the cooked tofu to the pan with the vegetables.

Prepare Sauce:

- In a small bowl, whisk together soy sauce, hoisin sauce, rice vinegar, and maple syrup or honey. Pour the sauce over the tofu and vegetables.

Toss and Cook:

- Toss everything together until the tofu and vegetables are evenly coated with the sauce. Cook for an additional 2-3 minutes.

Adjust Seasoning:

- Taste and adjust the seasoning, adding red pepper flakes for heat if desired.

Serve:

- Serve the stir-fry over cooked brown rice or quinoa.

Garnish:

- Garnish with chopped green onions and sesame seeds if desired.

Enjoy:

- Enjoy your Asian-Inspired Tofu Stir-Fry as a delicious and weight-conscious meal!

This stir-fry is not only nutritious but also versatile. You can customize the vegetables based on your preferences, and it's a great way to incorporate a variety of colorful veggies into your diet. Adjust the sauce ingredients according to your taste.

**Cauliflower Fried Rice:**

Ingredients:

- 1 medium-sized cauliflower, riced (you can use a food processor or box grater)
- 1 tablespoon vegetable oil or olive oil
- 2 cloves garlic, minced
- 1 teaspoon ginger, grated
- 1 cup mixed vegetables (peas, carrots, corn, diced bell peppers)
- 2 green onions, chopped
- 2 large eggs, beaten
- 3 tablespoons low-sodium soy sauce or tamari
- 1 tablespoon sesame oil
- Salt and pepper to taste
- Sesame seeds and chopped cilantro for garnish (optional)

Instructions:

Prepare Cauliflower Rice:

- Rice the cauliflower using a food processor or box grater to achieve a rice-like consistency.

Stir-Fry Vegetables:

- Heat vegetable oil in a large wok or skillet over medium-high heat. Add minced garlic and grated ginger, and sauté for about 30 seconds until fragrant.
- Add the mixed vegetables and cook for 3-4 minutes until they are tender-crisp.

Add Cauliflower Rice:

- Add the riced cauliflower to the pan. Stir well to combine with the vegetables.

Create Well in the Center:

- Push the cauliflower rice and vegetables to the sides of the pan, creating a well in the center.

Scramble Eggs:

- Pour the beaten eggs into the well. Allow them to set for a moment and then scramble them using a spatula until fully cooked.

Combine Everything:

- Mix the scrambled eggs with the cauliflower rice and vegetables.

Season:

- Drizzle soy sauce and sesame oil over the mixture. Stir well to evenly coat. Season with salt and pepper to taste.

Cook Through:

- Cook for an additional 3-4 minutes, stirring frequently, until the cauliflower is cooked through but still has a slight crunch.

Garnish and Serve:

- Garnish with chopped green onions, sesame seeds, and chopped cilantro if desired.

Enjoy:

- Serve your Cauliflower Fried Rice as a tasty and weight-conscious alternative to traditional fried rice!

This dish is rich in fiber and low in calories, making it a great option for those focusing on weight control. It's versatile, and you can customize it by adding protein sources like tofu, chicken, or shrimp if desired. Adjust the seasoning and ingredients to suit your taste preferences.

**Chickpea and Veggie Buddha Bowl:**

Ingredients:

For the Chickpeas:

- 1 can (15 oz) chickpeas, drained and rinsed
- 1 tablespoon olive oil
- 1 teaspoon ground cumin
- 1 teaspoon smoked paprika
- Salt and pepper to taste

For the Bowl:

- 2 cups cooked quinoa or brown rice
- 2 cups mixed vegetables (e.g., broccoli, bell peppers, cherry tomatoes, carrots), chopped
- 2 cups leafy greens (e.g., spinach, kale)
- 1 avocado, sliced
- 1 cucumber, sliced
- Hummus for serving
- Lemon wedges for serving

Instructions:

For the Chickpeas:

    Preheat Oven:
- Preheat the oven to 400°F (200°C).

Prepare Chickpeas:

- In a bowl, toss the chickpeas with olive oil, cumin, smoked paprika, salt, and pepper.

Roast Chickpeas:

- Spread the seasoned chickpeas on a baking sheet lined with parchment paper. Roast in the preheated oven for 20-25 minutes, or until they are crispy.

For the Bowl:

Prepare Vegetables:

- Steam or sauté the mixed vegetables until they are tender but still vibrant.

Assemble Buddha Bowl:

- In individual bowls, assemble the Buddha Bowl by placing a portion of cooked quinoa or brown rice, mixed vegetables, leafy greens, sliced avocado, and cucumber.

Add Roasted Chickpeas:

- Top the bowl with the roasted chickpeas for added protein and crunch.

Serve with Hummus:

- Serve the Buddha Bowl with a dollop of hummus on the side.

Squeeze Lemon:

- Squeeze fresh lemon juice over the bowl for extra flavor.

Enjoy:

- Enjoy your Chickpea and Veggie Buddha Bowl as a delicious and weight-conscious meal!

This Buddha Bowl is not only colorful and flavorful but also provides a good balance of macronutrients. Adjust the portion sizes based on your dietary needs and preferences.

Feel free to customize the bowl with your favorite vegetables and add herbs or spices for extra taste.

**Spinach and Feta Turkey Burgers:**

Ingredients:

- 1 pound lean ground turkey
- 1 cup fresh spinach, chopped
- 1/2 cup feta cheese, crumbled
- 1/4 cup red onion, finely chopped
- 1 clove garlic, minced
- 1 teaspoon dried oregano
- Salt and pepper to taste
- Whole wheat burger buns or lettuce wraps
- Toppings: lettuce, tomato, red onion, tzatziki sauce, etc.

Instructions:

Preheat Grill or Skillet:
- Preheat your grill or a skillet over medium-high heat.

Prepare Ingredients:
- In a large bowl, combine the lean ground turkey, chopped spinach, crumbled feta cheese, chopped red onion, minced garlic, dried oregano, salt, and pepper.

Mix Well:
- Mix the ingredients well until everything is evenly incorporated.

Form Patties:
- Divide the mixture into equal portions and form them into burger patties.

Cook Burgers:

- Grill the turkey burgers for about 5-6 minutes per side, or until they are fully cooked and reach an internal temperature of 165°F (74°C).

Toast Buns (Optional):

- If using burger buns, you can lightly toast them on the grill or in a toaster.

Assemble Burgers:

- Place each turkey burger on a bun or lettuce wrap.

Add Toppings:

- Add your favorite toppings such as lettuce, tomato, red onion, and a dollop of tzatziki sauce.

Serve:

- Serve the Spinach and Feta Turkey Burgers immediately.

Enjoy:

- Enjoy your delicious and weight-conscious turkey burgers!

These burgers are a healthier alternative to traditional beef burgers, providing lean protein and the added nutritional benefits of spinach and feta. Customize the toppings and use whole wheat buns or lettuce wraps for a lighter option. Adjust the seasoning according to your taste preferences.

**Zucchini Noodles with Pesto:**

Ingredients:

For the Zucchini Noodles:

- 4 medium-sized zucchini
- Salt

For the Pesto:

- 2 cups fresh basil leaves, packed
- 1/2 cup grated Parmesan cheese
- 1/3 cup pine nuts or walnuts
- 3 cloves garlic, minced
- 1/2 cup extra-virgin olive oil
- Salt and pepper to taste
- Juice of 1 lemon (optional)

Instructions:

For the Zucchini Noodles:

Spiralize Zucchini:
- Using a spiralizer, spiralize the zucchini into noodle-like shapes. If you don't have a spiralizer, you can use a vegetable peeler to create long, thin strips.

Salt Zucchini Noodles:

- Place the zucchini noodles in a colander, sprinkle with salt, and let them sit for about 10-15 minutes. This helps draw out excess moisture.

Rinse and Pat Dry:

- Rinse the salted zucchini noodles under cold water to remove the salt. Pat them dry with a clean kitchen towel or paper towels.

For the Pesto:

Prepare Pesto:

- In a food processor, combine the fresh basil, grated Parmesan cheese, pine nuts or walnuts, and minced garlic. Pulse until the ingredients are finely chopped.

Add Olive Oil:

- With the food processor running, slowly drizzle in the olive oil until the pesto reaches your desired consistency.

Season:

- Season the pesto with salt and pepper to taste. If you like a bit of tang, add the juice of one lemon and pulse to combine.

Assemble:

Toss Zucchini Noodles with Pesto:

- In a large bowl, toss the zucchini noodles with the prepared pesto until well coated.

Serve:

- Serve the Zucchini Noodles with Pesto immediately.

Optional Toppings:

- Optional toppings include additional grated Parmesan, cherry tomatoes, or a sprinkle of pine nuts.

Enjoy:

- Enjoy your Zucchini Noodles with Pesto as a light and delicious meal for weight control!

This dish is not only low in calories but also high in nutrients. Feel free to customize the pesto by adding other herbs like parsley or cilantro or incorporating spinach for an extra nutritional boost. Adjust the seasoning and lemon juice according to your taste preferences.

**Greek Salad with Grilled Shrimp:**

Ingredients:

For the Grilled Shrimp:

- 1 pound large shrimp, peeled and deveined
- 2 tablespoons olive oil
- 2 cloves garlic, minced
- 1 teaspoon dried oregano
- Salt and pepper to taste
- Lemon wedges for serving

For the Greek Salad:

- 4 cups mixed salad greens (romaine, spinach, arugula, etc.)
- 1 cucumber, sliced
- 1 cup cherry tomatoes, halved
- 1 red bell pepper, chopped
- 1/2 red onion, thinly sliced
- 1/2 cup Kalamata olives, pitted
- 1/2 cup crumbled feta cheese

For the Greek Dressing:

- 1/4 cup extra-virgin olive oil
- 2 tablespoons red wine vinegar
- 1 teaspoon Dijon mustard

- 1 teaspoon dried oregano
- Salt and pepper to taste

Instructions:

For the Grilled Shrimp:

Marinate Shrimp:
- In a bowl, combine shrimp with olive oil, minced garlic, dried oregano, salt, and pepper. Toss to coat the shrimp evenly. Let it marinate for about 15-30 minutes.

Grill Shrimp:
- Preheat the grill or a grill pan over medium-high heat. Thread the shrimp onto skewers if desired. Grill the shrimp for 2-3 minutes per side or until they are opaque and cooked through.

Serve with Lemon Wedges:
- Squeeze fresh lemon juice over the grilled shrimp and set aside.

For the Greek Salad:

Assemble Salad:
- In a large salad bowl, combine the mixed salad greens, sliced cucumber, cherry tomatoes, chopped red bell pepper, thinly sliced red onion, Kalamata olives, and crumbled feta cheese.

For the Greek Dressing:

Prepare Dressing:

- In a small bowl, whisk together the extra-virgin olive oil, red wine vinegar, Dijon mustard, dried oregano, salt, and pepper.

Toss Salad:

- Drizzle the Greek dressing over the salad and toss everything together until well coated.

Assemble and Serve:

Top with Grilled Shrimp:

- Arrange the grilled shrimp on top of the Greek salad.

Serve:

- Serve your Greek Salad with Grilled Shrimp immediately.

Enjoy:

- Enjoy this delicious and weight-conscious meal that's rich in flavors and nutrients!

Feel free to customize the salad with additional veggies like artichoke hearts, or sprinkle some chopped fresh herbs for added freshness. Adjust the dressing ingredients to suit your taste preferences.

# Dinner:

**Baked Salmon with Lemon and Dill:**

Ingredients:

- 4 salmon fillets (about 6 ounces each), skin-on or skinless
- Salt and pepper to taste
- 2 tablespoons olive oil
- 2 tablespoons fresh dill, chopped
- 1 lemon, thinly sliced
- 2 cloves garlic, minced (optional)
- Lemon wedges for serving

Instructions:

Preheat Oven:

- Preheat your oven to 375°F (190°C).

Prepare Salmon Fillets:

- Pat the salmon fillets dry with paper towels. Season both sides with salt and pepper.

Place Salmon on Baking Sheet:

- Place the salmon fillets on a baking sheet lined with parchment paper or lightly greased.

Drizzle with Olive Oil:

- Drizzle olive oil over the salmon fillets, ensuring they are evenly coated.

Sprinkle with Dill:

- Sprinkle chopped fresh dill over the salmon fillets. If you like, you can also add minced garlic for extra flavor.

Arrange Lemon Slices:

- Arrange lemon slices on top of the salmon fillets. This not only adds flavor but also helps keep the salmon moist during baking.

Bake:

- Bake in the preheated oven for approximately 12-15 minutes, or until the salmon is cooked through and flakes easily with a fork. Cooking time may vary depending on the thickness of your salmon fillets.

Serve:

- Carefully transfer the baked salmon to serving plates. Serve with additional lemon wedges on the side.

Enjoy:

- Enjoy your Baked Salmon with Lemon and Dill as a delicious and weight-conscious main course!

This dish is simple to prepare, light, and packed with healthy fats and protein. Adjust the seasoning and herb quantities according to your taste preferences. You can pair this salmon with a side of steamed vegetables or a fresh green salad for a well-balanced meal.

**Spaghetti Squash with Tomato Sauce:**

Ingredients:

For the Spaghetti Squash:

- 1 medium-sized spaghetti squash
- Olive oil
- Salt and pepper

For the Tomato Sauce:

- 2 tablespoons olive oil
- 1 onion, finely chopped
- 2 cloves garlic, minced
- 1 can (28 oz) crushed tomatoes
- 1 teaspoon dried oregano
- 1 teaspoon dried basil
- 1/2 teaspoon red pepper flakes (optional, for heat)
- Salt and pepper to taste
- Fresh basil or parsley for garnish (optional)
- Grated Parmesan cheese for serving (optional)

Instructions:

For the Spaghetti Squash:

Preheat Oven:
- Preheat your oven to 400°F (200°C).

Cut Squash:
- Carefully cut the spaghetti squash in half lengthwise. Scoop out the seeds and pulp with a spoon.

Season Squash:
- Drizzle olive oil over the cut sides of the spaghetti squash. Sprinkle with salt and pepper.

Roast Squash:
- Place the squash halves, cut side down, on a baking sheet lined with parchment paper. Roast in the preheated oven for about 40-50 minutes or until the squash is tender and can be easily pierced with a fork.

Scrape into "Noodles":
- Allow the squash to cool slightly, then use a fork to scrape the flesh into "noodles."

For the Tomato Sauce:

Sauté Onion and Garlic:
- In a saucepan, heat olive oil over medium heat. Add finely chopped onion and sauté until softened. Add minced garlic and cook for an additional 30 seconds.

Add Crushed Tomatoes and Seasonings:
- Pour in the crushed tomatoes and add dried oregano, dried basil, red pepper flakes (if using), salt, and pepper. Stir to combine.

Simmer:

- Allow the sauce to simmer over low heat for at least 20-30 minutes to let the flavors meld together. Stir occasionally.

Assemble:

Serve:
- Spoon the tomato sauce over the spaghetti squash "noodles."

Garnish and Enjoy:
- Garnish with fresh basil or parsley, and optionally, serve with grated Parmesan cheese. Enjoy your Spaghetti Squash with Tomato Sauce as a flavorful and weight-conscious meal!

This dish is not only delicious but also provides a lower-carb alternative to traditional pasta. It's versatile, and you can customize the tomato sauce with additional herbs or vegetables according to your preferences.

**Grilled Chicken Breast:**

Ingredients:

- 4 boneless, skinless chicken breasts
- 2 tablespoons olive oil
- 2 cloves garlic, minced
- 1 teaspoon dried oregano
- 1 teaspoon dried thyme
- Salt and pepper to taste
- Lemon wedges for serving

Instructions:

Prepare Chicken Marinade:
- In a bowl, mix olive oil, minced garlic, dried oregano, dried thyme, salt, and pepper to create a marinade.

Marinate Chicken:
- Coat the chicken breasts with the marinade, ensuring they are well-covered. Let them marinate for at least 30 minutes, or you can refrigerate for a few hours for more flavor.

Grill Chicken:

- Preheat the grill to medium-high heat. Grill the chicken breasts for about 6-7 minutes per side or until they reach an internal temperature of 165°F (74°C) and have nice grill marks.

Rest and Serve:

- Allow the grilled chicken to rest for a few minutes before serving. Serve with lemon wedges on the side.

Quinoa Pilaf:

Ingredients:

- 1 cup quinoa, rinsed and drained
- 2 cups low-sodium chicken or vegetable broth
- 1 tablespoon olive oil
- 1 small onion, finely chopped
- 2 carrots, diced
- 1 zucchini, diced
- 1 teaspoon ground cumin
- Salt and pepper to taste
- Fresh parsley for garnish (optional)

Instructions:

Cook Quinoa:

- In a saucepan, bring the broth to a boil. Add the rinsed quinoa, reduce heat to low, cover, and simmer for about 15 minutes or until the quinoa is cooked and the liquid is absorbed.

Sauté Vegetables:

- In a separate skillet, heat olive oil over medium heat. Add chopped onion, diced carrots, and diced zucchini. Sauté until the vegetables are tender.

Add Quinoa and Season:

- Add the cooked quinoa to the sautéed vegetables. Sprinkle ground cumin, salt, and pepper. Stir well to combine.

Garnish and Serve:

- Garnish with fresh parsley if desired. Serve the quinoa pilaf alongside the grilled chicken breast.

Enjoy:

- Enjoy your Grilled Chicken Breast with Quinoa Pilaf as a delicious and weight-conscious meal!

This dish is rich in protein, fiber, and essential nutrients. Adjust the seasonings and vegetables in the quinoa pilaf according to your preferences. It's a well-balanced meal that can be part of a healthy eating plan.

**Roasted Brussels Sprouts and Sweet Potatoes:**

Ingredients:

- 1 pound Brussels sprouts, trimmed and halved
- 2 medium-sized sweet potatoes, peeled and diced
- 3 tablespoons olive oil
- 1 teaspoon garlic powder
- 1 teaspoon smoked paprika
- Salt and pepper to taste
- Optional: 1/4 cup grated Parmesan cheese
- Optional: Chopped fresh herbs (such as rosemary or thyme) for garnish

Instructions:

Preheat Oven:
- Preheat your oven to 400°F (200°C).

Prepare Vegetables:
- In a large bowl, combine the halved Brussels sprouts and diced sweet potatoes.

Season with Olive Oil and Spices:
- Drizzle olive oil over the vegetables. Add garlic powder, smoked paprika, salt, and pepper. Toss the vegetables until evenly coated with the seasonings.

Spread on Baking Sheet:

- Spread the seasoned Brussels sprouts and sweet potatoes in a single layer on a baking sheet. Ensure they are not too crowded to allow for even roasting.

Roast in Oven:

- Roast in the preheated oven for about 25-30 minutes, or until the vegetables are golden brown and tender. Stir the vegetables halfway through the roasting time for even cooking.

Optional: Add Parmesan Cheese:

- If desired, sprinkle grated Parmesan cheese over the roasted vegetables during the last 5 minutes of cooking. This adds a delicious cheesy flavor.

Garnish and Serve:

- Garnish with chopped fresh herbs if you like.

Serve:

- Serve the Roasted Brussels Sprouts and Sweet Potatoes as a tasty and weight-conscious side dish.

Enjoy:

- Enjoy this nutritious and flavorful dish that provides a good balance of carbohydrates, fiber, and essential nutrients.

This recipe is not only suitable for weight control but also brings out the natural sweetness of the vegetables through roasting. Adjust the seasonings to suit your taste preferences, and feel free to get creative with additional herbs or spices.

**Stuffed Portobello Mushrooms with Quinoa:**

Ingredients:

- 4 large Portobello mushrooms, stems removed
- 1 cup quinoa, rinsed and drained
- 2 cups vegetable broth or water
- 1 tablespoon olive oil
- 1 small onion, finely chopped
- 2 cloves garlic, minced
- 1 red bell pepper, diced
- 1 zucchini, diced
- 1 cup cherry tomatoes, halved
- 1/2 cup crumbled feta cheese
- 1/4 cup chopped fresh parsley or basil
- Salt and pepper to taste
- Grated Parmesan cheese for topping (optional)
- Balsamic glaze for drizzling (optional)

Instructions:

Preheat Oven:

- Preheat your oven to 375°F (190°C).

Prepare Portobello Mushrooms:

- Clean the Portobello mushrooms and remove the stems. Place them on a baking sheet.

**Cook Quinoa:**

- In a saucepan, combine quinoa and vegetable broth (or water). Bring to a boil, then reduce the heat, cover, and simmer for about 15 minutes or until the quinoa is cooked and the liquid is absorbed. Fluff the quinoa with a fork.

**Sauté Vegetables:**

- In a large skillet, heat olive oil over medium heat. Add chopped onion and garlic, sautéing until softened. Add diced red bell pepper and zucchini, cooking for an additional 3-4 minutes. Stir in cherry tomatoes and cook for 1-2 minutes until they just start to soften.

**Combine Quinoa and Vegetables:**

- Add the cooked quinoa to the skillet with the sautéed vegetables. Mix well to combine.

**Season and Add Cheese:**

- Season the quinoa mixture with salt and pepper to taste. Stir in crumbled feta cheese and chopped fresh parsley or basil. Mix until the cheese is melted and the ingredients are well combined.

**Stuff Portobello Mushrooms:**

- Spoon the quinoa mixture into the Portobello mushroom caps, pressing down gently to pack the filling.

**Bake:**

- Bake in the preheated oven for about 20-25 minutes, or until the mushrooms are tender and the filling is heated through.

**Optional Toppings:**

- If desired, top each stuffed mushroom with grated Parmesan cheese and drizzle with balsamic glaze.

Serve:

- Serve the Stuffed Portobello Mushrooms with Quinoa as a delicious and weight-conscious meal.

Feel free to customize the filling with your favorite vegetables or herbs. This recipe is versatile and can be adapted based on your taste preferences. Enjoy your nutritious and flavorful stuffed mushrooms!

**Turkey Chili with Black Beans:**

Ingredients:

- 1 pound lean ground turkey
- 1 tablespoon olive oil
- 1 onion, diced
- 2 cloves garlic, minced
- 1 bell pepper, diced (any color)
- 1 jalapeño, finely chopped (optional, for heat)
- 1 can (15 oz) black beans, drained and rinsed
- 1 can (14 oz) diced tomatoes
- 1 can (6 oz) tomato paste
- 2 cups low-sodium chicken broth
- 2 teaspoons chili powder
- 1 teaspoon ground cumin
- 1 teaspoon paprika
- 1/2 teaspoon oregano
- Salt and pepper to taste
- Optional toppings: shredded cheese, chopped green onions, cilantro, plain Greek yogurt

Instructions:

Cook Ground Turkey:

- In a large pot, heat olive oil over medium heat. Add ground turkey and cook until browned, breaking it apart with a spoon as it cooks.

Sauté Vegetables:

- Add diced onion, minced garlic, diced bell pepper, and chopped jalapeño (if using) to the pot. Sauté until the vegetables are softened.

Add Spices:

- Stir in chili powder, ground cumin, paprika, oregano, salt, and pepper. Cook for 1-2 minutes to toast the spices.

Combine Beans and Tomatoes:

- Add black beans, diced tomatoes, tomato paste, and chicken broth to the pot. Stir to combine all ingredients.

Simmer:

- Bring the chili to a simmer, then reduce the heat to low. Cover and let it simmer for at least 20-30 minutes to allow the flavors to meld together.

Adjust Seasoning:

- Taste the chili and adjust the seasoning, adding more salt, pepper, or spices if needed.

Serve:

- Ladle the turkey chili into bowls. Top with shredded cheese, chopped green onions, cilantro, or a dollop of plain Greek yogurt if desired.

Enjoy:

- Enjoy your Turkey Chili with Black Beans as a filling and weight-conscious meal!

This turkey chili is not only delicious but also provides a good balance of protein and fiber. It's a versatile dish, and you can customize it with your favorite toppings and additional vegetables. Adjust the spice level according to your preference.

**Eggplant Parmesan with Whole Wheat Pasta:**

Ingredients:

For the Eggplant Parmesan:

- 1 large eggplant, sliced into 1/2-inch rounds
- Salt, for drawing out moisture
- 1 cup whole wheat breadcrumbs
- 1/2 cup grated Parmesan cheese
- 2 large eggs, beaten
- 2 cups marinara sauce (store-bought or homemade)
- 1 cup part-skim mozzarella cheese, shredded
- Fresh basil or parsley for garnish (optional)

For the Whole Wheat Pasta:

- 2 cups whole wheat pasta (spaghetti, penne, or your choice)
- Salt, for boiling

Instructions:

For the Eggplant Parmesan:

Preheat Oven:

- Preheat your oven to 375°F (190°C).

Slice and Salt Eggplant:

- Slice the eggplant into 1/2-inch rounds. Lay the slices on a paper towel-lined baking sheet, sprinkle with salt, and let them sit for about 30 minutes to draw out moisture.

Breading Station:

- In a shallow dish, combine whole wheat breadcrumbs and grated Parmesan cheese. Dip each eggplant slice into the beaten eggs, then coat with the breadcrumb mixture, pressing gently to adhere.

Bake Eggplant:

- Place the breaded eggplant slices on a baking sheet lined with parchment paper. Bake for about 20-25 minutes or until the eggplant is tender and golden brown.

Assemble Parmesan:

- In a baking dish, layer marinara sauce, baked eggplant slices, and shredded mozzarella cheese. Repeat the layers, finishing with a layer of mozzarella on top.

Bake Parmesan:

- Bake in the preheated oven for about 20-25 minutes or until the cheese is melted and bubbly.

For the Whole Wheat Pasta:

Cook Pasta:

- While the Eggplant Parmesan is baking, cook the whole wheat pasta according to the package instructions. Drain and set aside.

Serve:

Plate:

- Serve the baked Eggplant Parmesan over a bed of cooked whole wheat pasta.

Garnish:

- Garnish with fresh basil or parsley if desired.

Enjoy:

- Enjoy your Eggplant Parmesan with Whole Wheat Pasta as a delicious and weight-conscious meal!

This lighter version of Eggplant Parmesan retains all the flavors while reducing the calories. The whole wheat pasta adds fiber and nutrients to the dish. Adjust the seasoning and feel free to add extra herbs or spices to suit your taste preferences.

**Grilled Veggie Skewers with Tofu:**

Ingredients:

For the Tofu:

- 1 block extra-firm tofu, pressed and cubed
- 2 tablespoons soy sauce or tamari
- 1 tablespoon olive oil
- 1 teaspoon garlic powder
- 1 teaspoon smoked paprika
- Salt and pepper to taste

For the Veggie Skewers:

- 1 zucchini, sliced
- 1 bell pepper (any color), diced
- 1 red onion, diced
- Cherry tomatoes
- Mushrooms, cleaned and halved
- Wooden or metal skewers (if using wooden, soak them in water for 30 minutes)

For the Marinade:

- 3 tablespoons olive oil
- 2 tablespoons balsamic vinegar
- 1 teaspoon dried oregano
- 1 teaspoon dried thyme
- Salt and pepper to taste

Instructions:

For the Tofu:

Press Tofu:
- Press the tofu to remove excess water. Cut the tofu into cubes.

Marinate Tofu:
- In a bowl, combine soy sauce or tamari, olive oil, garlic powder, smoked paprika, salt, and pepper. Add the tofu cubes and let them marinate for at least 15-20 minutes.

Thread Tofu onto Skewers:
- Thread the marinated tofu cubes onto skewers.

For the Veggie Skewers:

Prepare Vegetables:
- In a separate bowl, whisk together olive oil, balsamic vinegar, dried oregano, dried thyme, salt, and pepper to create the marinade.

Marinate Vegetables:
- Toss the sliced zucchini, diced bell pepper, diced red onion, cherry tomatoes, and halved mushrooms in the marinade. Let them marinate for about 15 minutes.

Thread Vegetables onto Skewers:

- Thread the marinated vegetables onto separate skewers.

Grilling:

Preheat Grill:

- Preheat your grill to medium-high heat.

Grill Skewers:

- Grill the tofu skewers and vegetable skewers, turning occasionally, until the tofu is golden brown and the vegetables are tender and have nice grill marks.

Serve:

- Serve the Grilled Veggie Skewers with Tofu immediately.

Enjoy:

- Enjoy this delicious and weight-conscious meal!

These Grilled Veggie Skewers with Tofu are versatile, and you can customize the vegetables based on your preferences. This dish is not only healthy but also packed with flavors. Adjust the marinades and seasonings according to your taste.

**Cod Fish Tacos with Cabbage Slaw:**

Ingredients:

For the Cod Fish:

- 1 pound cod fillets, cut into small strips
- 1 tablespoon olive oil
- 1 teaspoon chili powder
- 1/2 teaspoon ground cumin
- 1/2 teaspoon garlic powder
- Salt and pepper to taste
- Juice of 1 lime

For the Cabbage Slaw:

- 2 cups shredded green cabbage
- 1/2 cup shredded carrot
- 1/4 cup chopped fresh cilantro
- 2 tablespoons plain Greek yogurt
- 1 tablespoon mayonnaise (optional)
- Juice of 1 lime
- Salt and pepper to taste

For Assembling Tacos:

- Corn or whole wheat tortillas
- Avocado slices

- Salsa or hot sauce (optional)
- Lime wedges for serving

Instructions:

For the Cod Fish:

Marinate Cod:

- In a bowl, combine olive oil, chili powder, ground cumin, garlic powder, salt, pepper, and lime juice. Add cod strips and toss to coat. Let it marinate for about 15-20 minutes.

Cook Cod:

- Heat a skillet over medium-high heat. Cook the marinated cod strips for about 2-3 minutes per side or until they are opaque and easily flake with a fork.

For the Cabbage Slaw:

Prepare Slaw:

- In a bowl, combine shredded green cabbage, shredded carrot, chopped cilantro, Greek yogurt, mayonnaise (if using), lime juice, salt, and pepper. Toss to combine.

Assembling Tacos:

Warm Tortillas:

- Warm the tortillas in a dry skillet or microwave according to the package instructions.

Assemble Tacos:

- Spoon some cabbage slaw onto each tortilla. Top with cooked cod strips.

Add Toppings:

- Add avocado slices on top, and drizzle with salsa or hot sauce if desired.

Garnish and Serve:

- Garnish with additional cilantro and serve with lime wedges on the side.

Enjoy:

- Enjoy your Cod Fish Tacos with Cabbage Slaw as a light and weight-conscious meal!

This recipe is a healthier alternative to traditional fried fish tacos, and the cabbage slaw adds a refreshing crunch. Feel free to customize the toppings and adjust the seasonings to suit your taste preferences.

## Snack:

**Hummus and Veggie Sticks:**

Ingredients:

For the Hummus:

- 1 can (15 oz) chickpeas, drained and rinsed
- 1/4 cup tahini
- 2 tablespoons olive oil
- 2 tablespoons lemon juice
- 2 cloves garlic, minced
- 1/2 teaspoon ground cumin
- Salt and pepper to taste
- Water (as needed for desired consistency)

For the Veggie Sticks:

- Carrot sticks
- Cucumber sticks
- Bell pepper strips (any color)
- Celery sticks
- Cherry tomatoes, halved
- Radish slices

Instructions:

For the Hummus:

Blend Ingredients:

- In a food processor, combine chickpeas, tahini, olive oil, lemon juice, minced garlic, ground cumin, salt, and pepper. Blend until smooth.

Adjust Consistency:

- If the hummus is too thick, add water a tablespoon at a time until you reach your desired consistency.

Taste and Adjust:

- Taste the hummus and adjust the seasonings as needed, adding more salt, pepper, or lemon juice if desired.

For the Veggie Sticks:

Prepare Vegetables:

- Wash and cut a variety of fresh vegetables into sticks or strips.

Assembling:

Serve:

- Arrange the veggie sticks on a plate alongside a bowl of the freshly made hummus.

Enjoy:

- Enjoy your Hummus and Veggie Sticks as a delicious and weight-conscious snack!

This snack is not only satisfying but also provides a good balance of protein, healthy fats, and fiber. It's a great option for those looking to maintain a healthy weight or simply enjoy a nutritious snack. Feel free to get creative with the vegetables and customize the hummus with additional herbs or spices.

**Greek Yogurt with Berries:**

Ingredients:

- 1 cup Greek yogurt (unsweetened)
- 1/2 cup mixed berries (such as strawberries, blueberries, raspberries, or blackberries)
- 1 tablespoon honey or maple syrup (optional, for sweetness)
- A sprinkle of chia seeds or granola (optional, for added texture)

Instructions:

Prepare the Berries:
- Wash the berries thoroughly and slice larger berries like strawberries if desired.

Assemble the Yogurt Bowl:
- Spoon Greek yogurt into a bowl or serving container.

Add Berries:
- Arrange the mixed berries on top of the Greek yogurt.

Drizzle Sweetener (Optional):
- If you prefer a sweeter taste, drizzle honey or maple syrup over the yogurt and berries. Adjust the sweetness to your liking.

Optional Toppings:
- Sprinkle chia seeds or granola over the yogurt for added texture and nutritional benefits.

Stir and Enjoy:

- If you like, you can gently stir the yogurt and berries together before eating. Enjoy this simple and delicious Greek Yogurt with Berries!

This snack is a great source of protein, vitamins, and antioxidants. It's versatile, and you can customize it with your favorite berries and toppings. Additionally, Greek yogurt adds a creamy texture and makes the snack more satisfying. Whether you enjoy it for breakfast, a snack, or a light dessert, Greek yogurt with berries is a wholesome and weight-conscious choice.

**Air-Popped Popcorn with Nutritional Yeast:**

Ingredients:

- 1/2 cup popcorn kernels
- 1-2 tablespoons nutritional yeast
- 1-2 tablespoons olive oil (optional)
- Salt to taste

Instructions:

Pop the Popcorn:

- Air-pop the popcorn using an air popper or your preferred method. If you don't have an air popper, you can pop the corn using a stovetop method with a little oil or use microwave popcorn without added butter.

Drizzle Olive Oil (Optional):

- If you like, drizzle a small amount of olive oil over the popped popcorn and toss to coat. This step is optional and can be omitted for a lower-calorie version.

Season with Nutritional Yeast:

- Sprinkle nutritional yeast over the popcorn while it's still warm. Toss the popcorn to ensure an even coating of nutritional yeast.

Salt to Taste:

- Add salt to taste. Nutritional yeast already adds a savory flavor, so adjust the salt according to your preference.

Toss and Serve:

- Toss the popcorn to evenly distribute the nutritional yeast and salt. Serve immediately.

Enjoy:

- Enjoy your Air-Popped Popcorn with Nutritional Yeast as a delicious and weight-conscious snack!

This snack is a healthier alternative to traditional buttered popcorn, and nutritional yeast provides a savory and cheesy flavor. Nutritional yeast is also a good source of protein and B-vitamins. Adjust the amount of nutritional yeast and salt based on your taste preferences. This snack is a great option for those looking for a satisfying yet low-calorie treat.

**Apple Slices with Almond Butter:**

Ingredients:

- 1 medium-sized apple (such as Fuji or Honeycrisp), cored and sliced
- 2 tablespoons almond butter (unsweetened)

Instructions:

Slice the Apple:

- Wash the apple and slice it into thin, even slices. You can leave the peel on for added fiber.

Serve with Almond Butter:

- Spread almond butter on each apple slice or use it as a dip for the apple slices.

Optional: Sprinkle with Cinnamon (Optional):

- If you like, sprinkle a bit of cinnamon on top for added flavor. Cinnamon complements the sweetness of the apple and the nutty taste of almond butter.

Enjoy:

- Enjoy your Apple Slices with Almond Butter as a delicious and weight-conscious snack!

This snack is not only satisfying but also provides a good balance of carbohydrates, healthy fats, and fiber. The natural sugars from the apple, combined with the protein and healthy fats from the almond butter, make for a tasty and wholesome treat. Adjust the portion size based on your dietary needs and preferences.

**Edamame with Sea Salt:**

Ingredients:

- 1 cup edamame (frozen or fresh)
- Sea salt, to taste

Instructions:

Cook Edamame:
- If using frozen edamame, cook them according to the package instructions. If using fresh edamame, you can steam or boil them until they are tender.

Season with Sea Salt:
- While the edamame is still warm, sprinkle sea salt over the pods. Toss or shake gently to ensure even coating.

Serve:
- Transfer the seasoned edamame to a serving bowl.

Enjoy:
- Enjoy your Edamame with Sea Salt as a delicious and weight-conscious snack!

Edamame is not only a good source of plant-based protein but also provides essential nutrients such as fiber, vitamins, and minerals. The sea salt adds a touch of flavor without adding many calories. Adjust the amount of salt based on your preference. This snack is not only satisfying but also a great option for those looking to maintain a healthy weight.

**Cottage Cheese with Pineapple:**

Ingredients:

- 1 cup cottage cheese (low-fat or full-fat, based on your preference)
- 1/2 cup fresh pineapple chunks or canned pineapple tidbits (drained)
- Optional: A drizzle of honey or a sprinkle of cinnamon (optional, for added sweetness or flavor)

Instructions:

Prepare Cottage Cheese:
- Place the desired amount of cottage cheese in a serving bowl.

Add Pineapple:
- Add fresh pineapple chunks or drained canned pineapple tidbits on top of the cottage cheese.

Optional Sweetener or Flavoring:
- If you like, drizzle a bit of honey over the cottage cheese and pineapple for added sweetness. Alternatively, sprinkle a bit of cinnamon for extra flavor.

Gently Mix (Optional):
- Gently mix the ingredients if you prefer a more even distribution of pineapple throughout the cottage cheese.

Serve:
- Serve immediately and enjoy your Cottage Cheese with Pineapple!

This snack is a great combination of protein from the cottage cheese and vitamins from the pineapple. It's a satisfying and balanced option for those looking for a healthy and weight-conscious snack. Adjust the portion sizes and optional ingredients based on your preferences and dietary needs.

**Trail Mix with Nuts and Dried Fruit:**

Ingredients:

- 1 cup mixed nuts (such as almonds, walnuts, cashews, or pistachios)
- 1/2 cup mixed dried fruits (such as raisins, cranberries, apricots, or figs)
- 1/4 cup seeds (such as pumpkin seeds or sunflower seeds)
- 1/4 cup dark chocolate chips or chunks (optional)
- 1/4 cup coconut flakes (optional)
- 1/2 teaspoon cinnamon (optional, for extra flavor)

Instructions:

Select Nuts and Dried Fruits:
- Choose a variety of nuts and dried fruits based on your preference. You can use raw or roasted nuts.

Combine Ingredients:
- In a bowl, combine the mixed nuts, dried fruits, seeds, dark chocolate chips or chunks (if using), and coconut flakes (if using).

Optional: Add Cinnamon (Optional):
- If you like, sprinkle cinnamon over the mixture for added flavor. Toss to evenly distribute.

Mix Thoroughly:
- Gently mix all the ingredients until well combined.

Portion into Snack Bags:
- Portion the trail mix into small snack-sized bags or containers for easy and controlled servings.

Store:
- Store the trail mix in an airtight container or individual bags.

Enjoy:
- Enjoy your Trail Mix with Nuts and Dried Fruit as a convenient and nutritious snack!

Trail mix is an excellent source of energy and provides a good balance of macronutrients. It's portable, making it a great on-the-go snack. Feel free to customize the mix based on your taste preferences and dietary restrictions. Adjust the portion sizes to meet your nutritional needs.

**Roasted Chickpeas with Paprika:**

Ingredients:

- 1 can (15 oz) chickpeas (garbanzo beans), drained and rinsed
- 1-2 tablespoons olive oil
- 1 teaspoon paprika
- 1/2 teaspoon garlic powder
- 1/2 teaspoon cumin
- Salt and pepper to taste

Instructions:

Preheat Oven:

- Preheat your oven to 400°F (200°C).

Dry Chickpeas:

- Drain and rinse the chickpeas thoroughly. Pat them dry with a paper towel to remove excess moisture.

Coat Chickpeas:

- In a bowl, toss the dried chickpeas with olive oil, paprika, garlic powder, cumin, salt, and pepper. Ensure that the chickpeas are well coated with the seasonings.

Spread on Baking Sheet:

- Spread the seasoned chickpeas in a single layer on a baking sheet lined with parchment paper.

Roast in the Oven:

- Roast the chickpeas in the preheated oven for about 20-30 minutes or until they become golden brown and crispy. Shake the pan or stir the chickpeas every 10 minutes for even roasting.

Cool:

- Allow the roasted chickpeas to cool for a few minutes before serving.

Enjoy:

- Enjoy your Roasted Chickpeas with Paprika as a delicious and crunchy snack!

Roasting chickpeas with paprika adds a smoky and slightly spicy flavor. They are a great alternative to traditional snacks and offer a good source of plant-based protein and fiber. Adjust the seasonings according to your taste preferences, and feel free to experiment with different spices and herbs. Store any leftovers in an airtight container for later enjoyment.

**Cucumber Slices with Tzatziki:**

Ingredients:

For the Tzatziki:

- 1 cup Greek yogurt
- 1 cucumber, finely diced or grated (seeded if necessary)
- 2 cloves garlic, minced
- 1 tablespoon fresh dill, chopped
- 1 tablespoon fresh mint, chopped (optional)
- 1 tablespoon olive oil
- 1 tablespoon lemon juice
- Salt and pepper to taste

For the Cucumber Slices:

- 2 English cucumbers, washed and sliced

Instructions:

For the Tzatziki:

Prepare Cucumber:
- If the cucumber has large seeds, you may want to scoop them out. Finely dice or grate the cucumber.

Drain Cucumber (Optional):

- Place the diced or grated cucumber in a fine mesh sieve or cheesecloth. Sprinkle with a pinch of salt and let it drain for about 15 minutes. This helps remove excess water from the cucumber.

Combine Ingredients:

- In a bowl, combine the Greek yogurt, drained cucumber, minced garlic, chopped dill, chopped mint (if using), olive oil, lemon juice, salt, and pepper. Mix well.

Chill:

- Refrigerate the tzatziki for at least 30 minutes to allow the flavors to meld.

For the Cucumber Slices:

Slice Cucumbers:

- Wash and slice the English cucumbers into thin rounds.

Assembling:

Top with Tzatziki:

- Place a small dollop of tzatziki on each cucumber slice.

Garnish (Optional):

- Garnish with additional fresh dill or mint if desired.

Serve:

- Serve your Cucumber Slices with Tzatziki as a refreshing and delightful appetizer or snack.

This snack is not only tasty but also a healthier option. It's low in calories, rich in vitamins, and offers a good balance of protein and hydration. Adjust the seasoning and ingredients based on your preferences. Enjoy this light and Greek-inspired treat!

**Hard-Boiled Eggs with Mustard:**

Ingredients:

- Hard-boiled eggs (as many as desired)
- Dijon mustard or your favorite mustard
- Salt and pepper to taste
- Optional: Fresh herbs or paprika for garnish

Instructions:

Hard-Boil Eggs:

- Hard-boil the eggs using your preferred method. You can use a stovetop, instant pot, or any method you are comfortable with.

Cool and Peel Eggs:

- Allow the hard-boiled eggs to cool completely. Once cooled, peel the eggs.

Slice Eggs:

- Slice each hard-boiled egg in half lengthwise.

Add Mustard:

- Place a small amount of mustard (Dijon or your preferred mustard) on top of each egg half. The amount can be adjusted based on your taste preferences.

Season:

- Sprinkle a pinch of salt and pepper over the eggs.

Garnish (Optional):

- If you like, garnish with fresh herbs like chives or a sprinkle of paprika for added flavor and presentation.

Serve:

- Arrange the hard-boiled eggs on a serving plate and serve immediately.

Enjoy:

- Enjoy your Hard-Boiled Eggs with Mustard as a simple and protein-rich snack!

This quick and easy snack is great for those who enjoy the combination of mustard with eggs. It's a good source of protein and healthy fats, making it a satisfying and nutritious choice. Adjust the amount of mustard and seasonings according to your taste preferences.

# Soups:

**Butternut Squash Soup:**

Ingredients:

- 1 medium-sized butternut squash, peeled, seeded, and diced
- 1 onion, chopped
- 2 carrots, peeled and chopped
- 2 apples, peeled, cored, and chopped
- 2 cloves garlic, minced
- 4 cups vegetable broth
- 1 teaspoon ground cinnamon
- 1/2 teaspoon ground nutmeg
- Salt and pepper to taste
- 2 tablespoons olive oil
- Optional toppings: Greek yogurt, pumpkin seeds, or fresh herbs for garnish

Instructions:

Prepare Ingredients:
- Peel, seed, and dice the butternut squash. Chop the onion, peel and chop the carrots, and peel, core, and chop the apples.

Sauté Vegetables:
- In a large pot, heat olive oil over medium heat. Add the chopped onion and garlic, and sauté until softened.

Add Squash, Carrots, and Apples:

- Add the diced butternut squash, chopped carrots, and apples to the pot. Cook for about 5 minutes, stirring occasionally.

Season:

- Season the vegetables with ground cinnamon, ground nutmeg, salt, and pepper. Stir to coat.

Add Broth:

- Pour in the vegetable broth, ensuring that the vegetables are well covered. Bring the mixture to a boil, then reduce the heat to low, cover, and simmer until the vegetables are tender (about 20-25 minutes).

Blend:

- Use an immersion blender to puree the soup until smooth. If you don't have an immersion blender, you can transfer the soup in batches to a blender, but be sure to let it cool slightly first.

Adjust Consistency:

- If the soup is too thick, add more vegetable broth until you reach your desired consistency.

Adjust Seasoning:

- Taste the soup and adjust the seasoning as needed.

Serve:

- Ladle the butternut squash soup into bowls. Garnish with a dollop of Greek yogurt, pumpkin seeds, or fresh herbs if desired.

Enjoy:

- Enjoy your delicious and warming Butternut Squash Soup!

This soup is not only flavorful but also packed with nutrients from the butternut squash, carrots, and apples. It's a versatile recipe, and you can adjust the seasonings and consistency based on your preferences. Serve it as a comforting meal on its own or as a starter to a larger meal.

**Minestrone Soup with Whole Wheat Pasta:**

Ingredients:

- 1 cup whole wheat pasta, uncooked
- 1 tablespoon olive oil
- 1 onion, diced
- 2 carrots, diced
- 2 celery stalks, diced
- 3 cloves garlic, minced
- 1 can (15 oz) diced tomatoes, undrained
- 1 can (15 oz) kidney beans, drained and rinsed
- 4 cups vegetable broth
- 2 teaspoons dried oregano
- 1 teaspoon dried basil
- 1 teaspoon dried thyme
- Salt and pepper to taste
- 2 cups chopped fresh spinach or kale
- Grated Parmesan cheese for serving (optional)

Instructions:

Cook Whole Wheat Pasta:

- Cook the whole wheat pasta according to the package instructions. Drain and set aside.

Sauté Vegetables:

- In a large pot, heat olive oil over medium heat. Add diced onion, carrots, celery, and minced garlic. Sauté until the vegetables are softened.

Add Tomatoes, Beans, and Broth:

- Add diced tomatoes (with their juice), kidney beans, vegetable broth, dried oregano, dried basil, dried thyme, salt, and pepper to the pot. Bring the soup to a boil, then reduce the heat to low and let it simmer for about 15-20 minutes.

Add Pasta and Greens:

- Stir in the cooked whole wheat pasta and chopped spinach or kale. Simmer for an additional 5-10 minutes until the greens are wilted and the pasta is heated through.

Adjust Seasoning:

- Taste the soup and adjust the seasoning, adding more salt and pepper if necessary.

Serve:

- Ladle the minestrone soup into bowls. Optionally, top each serving with grated Parmesan cheese.

Enjoy:

- Enjoy your wholesome Minestrone Soup with Whole Wheat Pasta!

This minestrone soup is not only delicious but also provides a good balance of carbohydrates, protein, and fiber. Whole wheat pasta adds a nutritious twist to the classic recipe. Feel free to customize the vegetables based on what you have on hand, and adjust the seasonings to suit your taste preferences.

**Chicken and Vegetable Soup:**

Ingredients:

- 1 pound boneless, skinless chicken breasts or thighs, diced
- 1 tablespoon olive oil
- 1 onion, diced
- 2 carrots, sliced
- 2 celery stalks, sliced
- 3 cloves garlic, minced
- 8 cups chicken broth (low-sodium)
- 1 cup diced tomatoes (fresh or canned)
- 1 cup green beans, chopped
- 1 cup corn kernels (fresh, frozen, or canned)
- 1 teaspoon dried thyme
- 1 teaspoon dried rosemary
- Salt and pepper to taste
- 1 cup pasta or rice (optional)
- Fresh parsley for garnish (optional)

Instructions:

Cook Chicken:

- In a large pot, heat olive oil over medium heat. Add diced chicken and cook until browned on all sides. Remove the chicken from the pot and set it aside.

Sauté Vegetables:

- In the same pot, add diced onion, sliced carrots, sliced celery, and minced garlic. Sauté until the vegetables are softened.

**Add Broth:**

- Pour in the chicken broth, scraping the bottom of the pot to release any browned bits. This adds flavor to the soup.

**Combine Ingredients:**

- Return the cooked chicken to the pot. Add diced tomatoes, chopped green beans, corn kernels, dried thyme, dried rosemary, salt, and pepper. Stir to combine.

**Simmer:**

- Bring the soup to a boil, then reduce the heat to low. Cover and simmer for about 20-25 minutes or until the vegetables are tender and the flavors meld.

**Add Pasta or Rice (Optional):**

- If you want to add pasta or rice, do so during the last 10-15 minutes of cooking, following the package instructions for the chosen ingredient.

**Adjust Seasoning:**

- Taste the soup and adjust the seasoning, adding more salt and pepper if necessary.

**Serve:**

- Ladle the chicken and vegetable soup into bowls. Garnish with fresh parsley if desired.

**Enjoy:**

- Enjoy your comforting and nutritious Chicken and Vegetable Soup!

This soup is customizable, and you can add your favorite vegetables or herbs. The addition of pasta or rice makes it a heartier meal. It's a great option for a wholesome and satisfying lunch or dinner.

**Gazpacho with Cucumber and Tomatoes:**

Ingredients:

- 6 ripe tomatoes, chopped
- 1 cucumber, peeled and chopped
- 1 red bell pepper, chopped
- 1 green bell pepper, chopped
- 1 small red onion, chopped
- 2 cloves garlic, minced
- 4 cups tomato juice
- 1/4 cup red wine vinegar
- 1/4 cup extra-virgin olive oil
- Salt and pepper to taste
- 1 teaspoon sugar (optional, to balance acidity)
- 1/2 teaspoon ground cumin
- 1/4 teaspoon cayenne pepper (optional, for a bit of heat)
- Fresh basil or cilantro for garnish (optional)
- Croutons for serving (optional)

Instructions:

Prepare Vegetables:

- Wash and chop the tomatoes, cucumber, red and green bell peppers, red onion, and garlic.

Blend Vegetables:

- In a blender or food processor, combine the chopped tomatoes, cucumber, bell peppers, red onion, and garlic. Pulse until the vegetables are finely chopped but not pureed.

Add Tomato Juice:

- Transfer the blended vegetables to a large bowl. Add tomato juice, red wine vinegar, extra-virgin olive oil, salt, pepper, sugar (if using), ground cumin, and cayenne pepper (if using).

Mix Well:

- Mix the ingredients well to combine. Adjust the seasoning according to your taste preferences.

Chill:

- Cover the bowl and refrigerate the gazpacho for at least 2 hours or until it's well-chilled.

Serve:

- Stir the gazpacho before serving. Ladle the chilled soup into bowls.

Garnish:

- Garnish with fresh basil or cilantro if desired. You can also add croutons for extra texture.

Enjoy:

- Enjoy your Gazpacho with Cucumber and Tomatoes as a refreshing and cooling soup!

Gazpacho is best served cold, making it a perfect summer dish. It's light, flavorful, and a great way to enjoy the bounty of fresh vegetables. Adjust the ingredients and seasonings to suit your taste.

**Quinoa and Kale Soup:**

Ingredients:

- 1 cup quinoa, rinsed
- 1 tablespoon olive oil
- 1 onion, diced
- 2 carrots, diced
- 2 celery stalks, diced
- 3 cloves garlic, minced
- 1 teaspoon ground cumin
- 1 teaspoon ground coriander
- 6 cups vegetable broth
- 1 can (15 oz) diced tomatoes, undrained
- 1 bunch kale, stems removed and leaves chopped
- Salt and pepper to taste
- Juice of 1 lemon
- Fresh parsley for garnish (optional)

Instructions:

Rinse Quinoa:
- Rinse quinoa under cold water. This helps remove the bitter coating.

Sauté Vegetables:
- In a large pot, heat olive oil over medium heat. Add diced onion, carrots, celery, and minced garlic. Sauté until the vegetables are softened.

Add Quinoa and Spices:

- Add rinsed quinoa to the pot. Stir in ground cumin and ground coriander. Cook for a couple of minutes to toast the quinoa and spices.

Pour in Broth:

- Pour in the vegetable broth and add the diced tomatoes (with their juice). Bring the soup to a boil.

Simmer:

- Reduce the heat to low, cover the pot, and let it simmer for about 15-20 minutes until the quinoa is cooked and the vegetables are tender.

Add Kale:

- Stir in the chopped kale and cook for an additional 5-7 minutes until the kale is wilted.

Season:

- Season the soup with salt, pepper, and lemon juice. Adjust the seasoning according to your taste.

Garnish:

- Garnish the soup with fresh parsley if desired.

Serve:

- Ladle the Quinoa and Kale Soup into bowls and serve hot.

Enjoy:

- Enjoy your nutritious and delicious Quinoa and Kale Soup!

This soup is not only packed with vitamins and minerals but also provides a good balance of protein and fiber from the quinoa and kale. Feel free to customize the recipe by adding other vegetables or herbs according to your preference.

**Black Bean Soup with Lime:**

Ingredients:

- 2 cans (15 oz each) black beans, drained and rinsed
- 1 tablespoon olive oil
- 1 onion, diced
- 2 bell peppers (any color), diced
- 2 carrots, diced
- 3 cloves garlic, minced
- 1 teaspoon ground cumin
- 1 teaspoon chili powder
- 4 cups vegetable broth
- 1 can (14 oz) diced tomatoes, undrained
- Juice of 2 limes
- Salt and pepper to taste
- Fresh cilantro for garnish (optional)
- Sour cream or Greek yogurt for topping (optional)

Instructions:

Sauté Vegetables:
- In a large pot, heat olive oil over medium heat. Add diced onion, bell peppers, carrots, and minced garlic. Sauté until the vegetables are softened.

Add Spices:

- Stir in ground cumin and chili powder. Cook for an additional 1-2 minutes to toast the spices.

Add Black Beans:

- Add the drained and rinsed black beans to the pot. Stir to combine with the vegetables and spices.

Pour in Broth and Tomatoes:

- Pour in the vegetable broth and add the diced tomatoes (with their juice). Bring the soup to a simmer.

Simmer:

- Reduce the heat to low, cover the pot, and let it simmer for about 20-25 minutes to allow the flavors to meld.

Blend (Optional):

- If you prefer a smoother soup, use an immersion blender to partially blend the soup. This step is optional, and you can leave the soup chunky if you prefer.

Add Lime Juice:

- Squeeze the juice of 2 limes into the soup. Stir well.

Season:

- Season the soup with salt and pepper to taste. Adjust the seasoning according to your preference.

Serve:

- Ladle the Black Bean Soup with Lime into bowls.

Garnish:

- Garnish with fresh cilantro if desired. You can also top each serving with a dollop of sour cream or Greek yogurt.

Enjoy:

- Enjoy your flavorful and zesty Black Bean Soup with Lime!

This soup is not only delicious but also a great source of protein and fiber from the black beans and an abundance of vitamins from the vegetables. Adjust the spice level and acidity to suit your taste. Serve it with crusty bread or tortilla chips for a complete meal.

**Tomato Basil Soup with Chickpeas:**

Ingredients:

- 2 tablespoons olive oil
- 1 onion, diced
- 3 cloves garlic, minced
- 2 cans (28 oz each) diced tomatoes
- 1 can (15 oz) chickpeas, drained and rinsed
- 4 cups vegetable broth
- 1 teaspoon dried basil
- 1/2 teaspoon dried oregano
- Salt and pepper to taste
- 1/4 teaspoon red pepper flakes (optional, for heat)
- 1/2 cup fresh basil leaves, chopped
- 1/2 cup heavy cream or coconut milk (optional, for creaminess)
- Grated Parmesan cheese for serving (optional)

Instructions:

Sauté Vegetables:
- In a large pot, heat olive oil over medium heat. Add diced onion and sauté until softened.

Add Garlic:
- Add minced garlic to the pot and sauté for an additional 1-2 minutes until fragrant.

Add Tomatoes and Chickpeas:

- Pour in the diced tomatoes (with their juice) and add the drained and rinsed chickpeas. Stir to combine.

Add Broth and Seasonings:

- Pour in the vegetable broth. Add dried basil, dried oregano, salt, pepper, and red pepper flakes (if using). Stir well.

Simmer:

- Bring the soup to a simmer, then reduce the heat to low. Cover the pot and let it simmer for about 15-20 minutes to allow the flavors to meld.

Blend (Optional):

- If you prefer a smoother soup, use an immersion blender to partially blend the soup. This step is optional, and you can leave the soup chunky if you prefer.

Add Fresh Basil:

- Stir in the chopped fresh basil leaves.

Add Cream (Optional):

- If using, add the heavy cream or coconut milk to the soup for added creaminess. Stir well.

Adjust Seasoning:

- Taste the soup and adjust the seasoning, adding more salt and pepper if necessary.

Serve:

- Ladle the Tomato Basil Soup with Chickpeas into bowls.

Garnish:

- Optionally, garnish each serving with grated Parmesan cheese.

Enjoy:

- Enjoy your delicious and wholesome Tomato Basil Soup with Chickpeas!

This soup is perfect for a comforting meal, especially on cooler days. The chickpeas add a protein boost, and the combination of tomatoes and basil provides a classic and satisfying flavor. Adjust the seasonings and ingredients based on your preferences. Serve with crusty bread or a side salad for a complete meal.

**Miso Soup with Tofu and Seaweed:**

Ingredients:

- 4 cups dashi (Japanese soup stock) or vegetable broth
- 3 tablespoons white miso paste
- 1 cup firm tofu, cubed
- 1 sheet nori (seaweed), cut into thin strips or torn into small pieces
- 2 green onions, thinly sliced
- 1 tablespoon soy sauce (optional, for additional flavor)
- 1 teaspoon sesame oil (optional, for added richness)
- Pinch of white pepper (optional)
- Chopped fresh cilantro or parsley for garnish (optional)

Instructions:

Prepare Tofu:
- Cut the firm tofu into small cubes.

Prepare Seaweed:
- Cut or tear the nori (seaweed) into thin strips or small pieces.

Make Dashi or Heat Broth:
- If using dashi, prepare it according to the package instructions. Alternatively, heat vegetable broth in a pot.

Dissolve Miso Paste:
- In a small bowl, dissolve the white miso paste in a few tablespoons of the hot dashi or broth, stirring until smooth.

Add Miso to Broth:

- Add the dissolved miso paste to the pot with the remaining dashi or broth. Stir well to combine.

Add Tofu and Nori:

- Add the cubed tofu and nori strips to the soup. Let it simmer over low heat for about 5-7 minutes until the tofu is heated through and the nori becomes tender.

Season:

- Optionally, add soy sauce, sesame oil, and white pepper for additional flavor. Adjust the seasoning to your taste.

Add Green Onions:

- Add thinly sliced green onions to the soup just before serving.

Garnish (Optional):

- Garnish the Miso Soup with Tofu and Seaweed with chopped fresh cilantro or parsley if desired.

Serve:

- Ladle the soup into bowls and serve hot.

Enjoy:

- Enjoy your delicious and nourishing Miso Soup with Tofu and Seaweed!

This miso soup is not only tasty but also a good source of protein and minerals. Feel free to customize it by adding other ingredients like mushrooms, spinach, or bean sprouts. Adjust the seasonings according to your preferences. Serve it as a comforting appetizer or as part of a Japanese-inspired meal.

**Lentil and Spinach Soup:**

Ingredients:

- 1 cup dried green or brown lentils, rinsed and drained
- 1 tablespoon olive oil
- 1 onion, finely chopped
- 3 carrots, peeled and diced
- 3 celery stalks, diced
- 3 cloves garlic, minced
- 1 teaspoon ground cumin
- 1 teaspoon ground coriander
- 1/2 teaspoon turmeric (optional)
- 6 cups vegetable broth
- 1 can (14 oz) diced tomatoes, undrained
- 2 cups fresh spinach, chopped
- Salt and pepper to taste
- Juice of 1 lemon
- Fresh parsley for garnish (optional)
- Crusty bread for serving (optional)

Instructions:

Rinse Lentils:

- Rinse the lentils under cold water and drain.

Sauté Vegetables:

- In a large pot, heat olive oil over medium heat. Add chopped onion, diced carrots, and diced celery. Sauté until the vegetables are softened.

Add Garlic and Spices:

- Add minced garlic, ground cumin, ground coriander, and turmeric (if using). Cook for an additional 1-2 minutes until fragrant.

Add Lentils and Broth:

- Stir in the rinsed lentils, vegetable broth, and diced tomatoes (with their juice). Bring the soup to a boil.

Simmer:

- Reduce the heat to low, cover the pot, and let it simmer for about 25-30 minutes or until the lentils are tender.

Add Spinach:

- Stir in the chopped fresh spinach and cook for an additional 5 minutes until the spinach wilts.

Season:

- Season the soup with salt and pepper to taste. Adjust the seasoning according to your preference.

Add Lemon Juice:

- Squeeze the juice of 1 lemon into the soup. Stir well.

Garnish (Optional):

- Optionally, garnish the Lentil and Spinach Soup with fresh parsley.

Serve:

- Ladle the soup into bowls and serve hot.

Enjoy:

- Enjoy your wholesome and delicious Lentil and Spinach Soup! Serve with crusty bread if desired.

This soup is not only rich in protein from the lentils but also packed with vitamins and minerals from the vegetables. It's a comforting and satisfying meal that's perfect for lunch or dinner. Adjust the ingredients and seasonings based on your preferences.

**Creamy Broccoli Soup with Greek Yogurt:**

Ingredients:

- 2 tablespoons olive oil
- 1 onion, chopped
- 3 cloves garlic, minced
- 4 cups broccoli florets
- 1 potato, peeled and diced
- 4 cups vegetable broth
- Salt and pepper to taste
- 1 cup Greek yogurt
- 1 tablespoon lemon juice
- Optional toppings: Croutons, grated cheddar cheese, or additional Greek yogurt for serving

Instructions:

Sauté Vegetables:
- In a large pot, heat olive oil over medium heat. Add chopped onion and minced garlic. Sauté until the onion is softened.

Add Broccoli and Potato:
- Add broccoli florets and diced potato to the pot. Stir to combine with the onions and garlic.

Pour in Broth:
- Pour in the vegetable broth. Bring the mixture to a boil.

Simmer:

- Reduce the heat to low, cover the pot, and let it simmer for about 15-20 minutes or until the broccoli and potato are tender.

Blend:
- Use an immersion blender to blend the soup until smooth. Alternatively, transfer the soup to a blender in batches, blending until smooth. Be cautious when blending hot liquids.

Season:
- Season the soup with salt and pepper to taste. Adjust the seasoning according to your preference.

Add Greek Yogurt and Lemon Juice:
- Stir in Greek yogurt and lemon juice. Mix well until the yogurt is fully incorporated into the soup.

Reheat (Optional):
- If needed, gently reheat the soup on low heat. Be careful not to boil it after adding the yogurt.

Serve:
- Ladle the Creamy Broccoli Soup into bowls.

Top (Optional):
- Optionally, top each serving with croutons, grated cheddar cheese, or an additional dollop of Greek yogurt.

Enjoy:
- Enjoy your delicious and creamy Broccoli Soup with Greek Yogurt!

This soup is a great way to enjoy the goodness of broccoli with the creaminess of Greek yogurt. It's a satisfying and wholesome meal, perfect for lunch or a light dinner.

Customize it with your favorite toppings and serve with crusty bread for a complete experience.

# Salads:

**Kale and Quinoa Salad with Cranberries:**

Ingredients:

- 1 cup quinoa, rinsed
- 2 cups water or vegetable broth
- 1 bunch kale, stems removed and leaves thinly sliced
- 1/2 cup dried cranberries
- 1/2 cup feta cheese, crumbled
- 1/4 cup sliced almonds, toasted
- 1/4 cup extra-virgin olive oil
- 2 tablespoons balsamic vinegar
- 1 tablespoon Dijon mustard
- 1 clove garlic, minced
- Salt and pepper to taste

Instructions:

Cook Quinoa:

- In a medium saucepan, combine quinoa and water or vegetable broth. Bring to a boil, then reduce the heat to low, cover, and simmer for about 15 minutes or until the quinoa is cooked and water is absorbed. Fluff the quinoa with a fork and let it cool.

Prepare Kale:

- Wash the kale leaves thoroughly, remove the stems, and thinly slice the leaves.

Massage Kale:

- Place the sliced kale in a large bowl. Drizzle with a bit of olive oil and massage the kale with your hands for a few minutes. This helps to soften the kale.

Assemble Salad:

- Add the cooked quinoa, dried cranberries, crumbled feta cheese, and toasted sliced almonds to the bowl with the kale.

Prepare Dressing:

- In a small bowl, whisk together olive oil, balsamic vinegar, Dijon mustard, minced garlic, salt, and pepper to make the dressing.

Dress Salad:

- Pour the dressing over the salad and toss everything together until well combined.

Chill (Optional):

- If you have time, refrigerate the salad for about 30 minutes before serving to allow the flavors to meld.

Serve:

- Serve the Kale and Quinoa Salad with Cranberries as a refreshing and nutritious side dish or a light main course.

Enjoy:

- Enjoy your vibrant and tasty Kale and Quinoa Salad with Cranberries!

This salad is not only visually appealing but also packed with nutrients from kale and quinoa. The combination of sweet cranberries, salty feta, and crunchy almonds adds wonderful texture and flavor. Adjust the dressing ingredients to your taste and feel free to add other vegetables or herbs for extra freshness.

**Caprese Salad with Balsamic Glaze:**

Ingredients:

- 4 large tomatoes, sliced
- 8 ounces fresh mozzarella cheese, sliced
- Fresh basil leaves
- Salt and pepper to taste
- Extra-virgin olive oil for drizzling
- Balsamic glaze for drizzling

Instructions:

Slice Tomatoes and Mozzarella:
- Wash and slice the tomatoes and fresh mozzarella into approximately 1/4-inch thick slices.

Arrange on a Platter:
- Arrange the tomato and mozzarella slices alternately on a serving platter.

Layer with Basil:
- Place fresh basil leaves between the tomato and mozzarella slices. You can use whole leaves or chiffonade (thinly sliced) basil.

Season:
- Sprinkle salt and pepper over the tomato and mozzarella slices to taste.

Drizzle with Olive Oil:
- Drizzle extra-virgin olive oil over the Caprese salad for added flavor.

Drizzle with Balsamic Glaze:

- Generously drizzle balsamic glaze over the salad. The balsamic glaze adds a sweet and tangy flavor that complements the freshness of the ingredients.

Serve:

- Serve the Caprese Salad with Balsamic Glaze immediately as a refreshing appetizer or side dish.

Enjoy:

- Enjoy the classic flavors of tomatoes, fresh mozzarella, and basil in this simple and elegant Caprese salad!

This salad is best enjoyed when tomatoes are in season for maximum flavor. The balsamic glaze adds a delightful sweetness that enhances the overall taste of the salad. It's a great dish for summer gatherings or as a light and flavorful starter.

**Watermelon and Feta Salad:**

Ingredients:

- 4 cups seedless watermelon, cubed
- 1 cup feta cheese, crumbled
- 1/2 cup red onion, thinly sliced
- 1/4 cup fresh mint leaves, chopped
- 1/4 cup extra-virgin olive oil
- 2 tablespoons balsamic glaze
- Salt and pepper to taste

Instructions:

Prepare Watermelon:

- Cut the seedless watermelon into bite-sized cubes. If you don't have seedless watermelon, be sure to remove the seeds.

Crumble Feta:

- Crumble the feta cheese into small pieces.

Slice Red Onion:

- Thinly slice the red onion.

Chop Fresh Mint:

- Chop the fresh mint leaves.

Assemble Salad:

- In a large bowl, combine the cubed watermelon, crumbled feta cheese, sliced red onion, and chopped fresh mint.

Drizzle Olive Oil:

- Drizzle extra-virgin olive oil over the salad.

Season:

- Season the salad with salt and pepper to taste.

Gently Toss:

- Gently toss all the ingredients together to ensure they are evenly coated with the olive oil and seasonings.

Drizzle with Balsamic Glaze:

- Drizzle balsamic glaze over the Watermelon and Feta Salad. The balsamic glaze adds a sweet and tangy flavor.

Serve:

- Serve the salad immediately as a refreshing and light side dish or appetizer.

Enjoy:

- Enjoy the delicious contrast of sweet watermelon, salty feta, and the burst of freshness from mint in this Watermelon and Feta Salad!

This salad is perfect for summer and is a great addition to picnics, barbecues, or any outdoor gatherings. The combination of juicy watermelon, creamy feta, and the aromatic touch of mint makes it a crowd-pleaser. Adjust the quantities and ingredients based on your preferences.

**Roasted Beet Salad with Goat Cheese:**

Ingredients:

- 4 medium-sized beets, washed and trimmed
- 2 tablespoons olive oil
- Salt and pepper to taste
- 4 cups mixed salad greens (e.g., arugula, spinach, or mixed baby greens)
- 1/2 cup goat cheese, crumbled
- 1/4 cup walnuts, toasted and chopped
- Balsamic glaze for drizzling (optional)
- Honey for drizzling (optional)

Instructions:

Roast Beets:

- Preheat the oven to 400°F (200°C).
- Place the washed and trimmed beets on a baking sheet. Drizzle with olive oil and season with salt and pepper. Toss to coat evenly.
- Roast in the preheated oven for about 45-60 minutes or until the beets are tender when pierced with a fork. The roasting time may vary depending on the size of the beets.

Cool and Peel Beets:

- Allow the roasted beets to cool. Once they are cool enough to handle, peel off the skin. The skin should easily rub off, or you can use a knife.

Slice Beets:

- Slice the roasted beets into thin rounds or wedges.

Assemble Salad:

- Arrange the mixed salad greens on a serving platter.
- Place the sliced roasted beets on top of the greens.

Add Goat Cheese and Walnuts:

- Sprinkle crumbled goat cheese and toasted, chopped walnuts over the beets.

Drizzle with Balsamic Glaze and Honey (Optional):

- Drizzle the salad with balsamic glaze for a sweet and tangy flavor. You can also add a touch of honey for extra sweetness.

Serve:

- Serve the Roasted Beet Salad with Goat Cheese immediately as a vibrant and delicious salad.

Enjoy:

- Enjoy the delightful combination of roasted beets, creamy goat cheese, and crunchy walnuts in this refreshing salad!

This salad makes a wonderful side dish or a light lunch. The flavors and textures work together beautifully, and the addition of balsamic glaze and honey enhances the overall taste. Adjust the quantities and ingredients according to your preferences.

**Caesar Salad with Grilled Chicken:**

Ingredients:

*For the Caesar Dressing:*

- 1/2 cup mayonnaise
- 2 tablespoons Dijon mustard
- 2 cloves garlic, minced
- 2 anchovy fillets, minced (or 1 tablespoon anchovy paste)
- 1 tablespoon Worcestershire sauce
- 1 tablespoon red wine vinegar
- Juice of 1 lemon
- 1/2 cup grated Parmesan cheese
- Salt and black pepper to taste

*For the Salad:*

- 2 boneless, skinless chicken breasts
- Salt and black pepper to season chicken
- 1 tablespoon olive oil (for grilling)
- 1 large head romaine lettuce, washed and chopped
- 1 cup croutons
- 1/2 cup grated Parmesan cheese (for salad)
- Lemon wedges for serving (optional)

Instructions:

Prepare the Caesar Dressing:
- In a bowl, whisk together mayonnaise, Dijon mustard, minced garlic, minced anchovies (or anchovy paste), Worcestershire sauce, red wine vinegar, lemon juice, and grated Parmesan cheese.
- Season with salt and black pepper to taste. Adjust the seasoning as needed. Refrigerate until ready to use.

Grill the Chicken:
- Season the chicken breasts with salt and black pepper.
- Heat a grill or grill pan over medium-high heat. Brush the chicken with olive oil.
- Grill the chicken for about 6-8 minutes per side or until cooked through and grill marks appear. The internal temperature should reach 165°F (74°C).
- Allow the chicken to rest for a few minutes before slicing.

Assemble the Salad:
- In a large salad bowl, toss the chopped romaine lettuce with the Caesar dressing until well coated.
- Add croutons and toss again.
- Divide the dressed salad among serving plates.

Slice Grilled Chicken:
- Slice the grilled chicken breasts into thin strips.

Top with Chicken and Parmesan:
- Arrange the sliced grilled chicken on top of each salad.
- Sprinkle grated Parmesan cheese over the salads.

Serve:
- Optionally, garnish with additional croutons and lemon wedges.

- Serve the Caesar Salad with Grilled Chicken immediately.

Enjoy:

- Enjoy this classic and satisfying Caesar Salad with the added goodness of grilled chicken!

This recipe provides a delicious balance of flavors and textures. The grilled chicken adds protein and a smoky flavor to the classic Caesar Salad. Customize the salad by adjusting the dressing's consistency and adjusting the quantity of croutons and Parmesan cheese according to your preference.

**Mango Avocado Salad with Lime Dressing:**

Ingredients:

*For the Salad:*

- 2 ripe mangoes, peeled, pitted, and diced
- 2 ripe avocados, peeled, pitted, and diced
- 1/4 cup red onion, finely chopped
- 1/4 cup fresh cilantro, chopped
- 1/4 cup feta cheese, crumbled (optional)
- Mixed salad greens (e.g., arugula or spinach)

*For the Lime Dressing:*

- 3 tablespoons olive oil
- Juice of 2 limes
- 1 teaspoon honey or maple syrup
- Salt and black pepper to taste

Instructions:

Prepare the Lime Dressing:
- In a small bowl, whisk together olive oil, lime juice, honey or maple syrup, salt, and black pepper. Adjust the sweetness and seasoning according to your taste. Set aside.

Assemble the Salad:

- In a large salad bowl, combine diced mangoes, diced avocados, chopped red onion, and chopped cilantro.
- If using, add crumbled feta cheese to the salad.

Add Greens:

- Add a handful of mixed salad greens to the bowl.

Drizzle with Lime Dressing:

- Drizzle the lime dressing over the salad ingredients.

Toss Gently:

- Gently toss the salad until all ingredients are well coated with the lime dressing.

Serve:

- Serve the Mango Avocado Salad over additional mixed greens or as is.

Optional Garnish:

- Optionally, garnish with additional cilantro or a sprinkle of feta cheese.

Enjoy:

- Enjoy the vibrant and tropical flavors of this Mango Avocado Salad with Lime Dressing!

This salad is perfect for a light and refreshing side dish, or you can enjoy it as a standalone meal. The combination of sweet mangoes, creamy avocados, and the zesty lime dressing creates a delicious and satisfying salad. Adjust the ingredients and dressing according to your preferences.

**Asian Cabbage Salad with Sesame Ginger Dressing:**

Ingredients:

*For the Salad:*

- 4 cups shredded green cabbage
- 1 cup shredded red cabbage
- 1 cup shredded carrots
- 1 red bell pepper, thinly sliced
- 1 cup edamame, cooked and cooled
- 1/4 cup chopped green onions
- 1/4 cup chopped fresh cilantro
- 1/4 cup sliced almonds, toasted
- 1 tablespoon sesame seeds, toasted

*For the Sesame Ginger Dressing:*

- 3 tablespoons soy sauce
- 2 tablespoons rice vinegar
- 1 tablespoon sesame oil
- 1 tablespoon honey or maple syrup
- 1 tablespoon freshly grated ginger
- 1 clove garlic, minced
- 1/4 cup neutral-flavored oil (vegetable or canola oil)
- Salt and black pepper to taste

Instructions:

Prepare the Sesame Ginger Dressing:

- In a small bowl, whisk together soy sauce, rice vinegar, sesame oil, honey or maple syrup, grated ginger, minced garlic, and neutral-flavored oil. Season with salt and black pepper to taste. Set aside.

Assemble the Salad:

- In a large salad bowl, combine shredded green cabbage, shredded red cabbage, shredded carrots, sliced red bell pepper, edamame, chopped green onions, and chopped fresh cilantro.

Toss with Dressing:

- Drizzle the Sesame Ginger Dressing over the salad ingredients.

Toss Gently:

- Gently toss the salad until all ingredients are well coated with the dressing.

Toast Almonds and Sesame Seeds:

- In a dry pan over medium heat, toast sliced almonds and sesame seeds until golden brown. Keep a close eye on them, as they can burn quickly.

Add Toasted Almonds and Sesame Seeds:

- Sprinkle the toasted almonds and sesame seeds over the salad.

Serve:

- Serve the Asian Cabbage Salad immediately, or refrigerate until ready to serve.

Enjoy:

- Enjoy the crisp and flavorful Asian Cabbage Salad with Sesame Ginger Dressing as a side dish or a light and refreshing main course!

This salad is not only visually appealing but also packed with vibrant colors and textures. The sesame ginger dressing adds a wonderful Asian-inspired flavor.

Customize the salad by adding protein like grilled chicken or tofu if desired. Adjust the dressing ingredients to suit your taste preferences.

**Greek Salad with Quinoa:**

Ingredients:

*For the Salad:*

- 1 cup cooked quinoa, cooled
- 1 cucumber, diced
- 1 cup cherry tomatoes, halved
- 1 bell pepper (red, yellow, or green), diced
- 1/2 cup red onion, thinly sliced
- 1/2 cup Kalamata olives, pitted
- 1/2 cup crumbled feta cheese
- 1/4 cup fresh parsley, chopped

*For the Dressing:*

- 1/4 cup extra-virgin olive oil
- 2 tablespoons red wine vinegar
- 1 teaspoon dried oregano
- Salt and black pepper to taste

Instructions:

Prepare Quinoa:
- Cook quinoa according to package instructions. Allow it to cool to room temperature.

Chop Vegetables:

- Dice the cucumber, halve the cherry tomatoes, dice the bell pepper, thinly slice the red onion, and chop the fresh parsley.

Assemble Salad:

- In a large salad bowl, combine the cooked and cooled quinoa with the diced cucumber, halved cherry tomatoes, diced bell pepper, sliced red onion, Kalamata olives, crumbled feta cheese, and chopped fresh parsley.

Prepare Dressing:

- In a small bowl, whisk together extra-virgin olive oil, red wine vinegar, dried oregano, salt, and black pepper to make the dressing.

Toss with Dressing:

- Drizzle the dressing over the salad ingredients.

Toss Gently:

- Gently toss the salad until all ingredients are well coated with the dressing.

Chill (Optional):

- Refrigerate the Greek Salad with Quinoa for about 30 minutes to let the flavors meld.

Serve:

- Serve the salad as a side dish or a light main course.

Enjoy:

- Enjoy the delightful combination of Greek flavors with the added nutritional boost from quinoa!

This Greek Salad with Quinoa is a perfect meal for lunch or dinner, providing a mix of textures and flavors. The quinoa adds protein and fiber, making the salad more satisfying. Feel free to customize the salad by adding or omitting ingredients based on your preferences.

**Spinach and Strawberry Salad:**

Ingredients:

*For the Salad:*

- 6 cups fresh baby spinach, washed and dried
- 1 1/2 cups fresh strawberries, hulled and sliced
- 1/2 cup red onion, thinly sliced
- 1/2 cup crumbled feta cheese
- 1/4 cup sliced almonds, toasted

*For the Dressing:*

- 3 tablespoons extra-virgin olive oil
- 2 tablespoons balsamic vinegar
- 1 tablespoon honey or maple syrup
- 1 teaspoon Dijon mustard
- Salt and black pepper to taste

Instructions:

Prepare Salad Ingredients:

- Wash and dry the baby spinach. Hull and slice the fresh strawberries. Thinly slice the red onion. Toast the sliced almonds in a dry pan over medium heat until golden brown.

Assemble Salad:

- In a large salad bowl, combine the baby spinach, sliced strawberries, sliced red onion, crumbled feta cheese, and toasted sliced almonds.

Prepare Dressing:

- In a small bowl, whisk together extra-virgin olive oil, balsamic vinegar, honey or maple syrup, Dijon mustard, salt, and black pepper to make the dressing.

Toss with Dressing:

- Drizzle the dressing over the salad ingredients.

Toss Gently:

- Gently toss the salad until all ingredients are well coated with the dressing.

Chill (Optional):

- Refrigerate the Spinach and Strawberry Salad for about 15 minutes to allow the flavors to meld.

Serve:

- Serve the salad as a refreshing side dish or a light main course.

Enjoy:

- Enjoy the vibrant colors and flavors of this Spinach and Strawberry Salad!

This salad is perfect for warm weather and makes a lovely addition to picnics, barbecues, or as a light and healthy lunch. The combination of sweet strawberries, savory feta, and crunchy almonds creates a delightful balance. Adjust the dressing ingredients to suit your taste preferences.

**Tuna Salad Lettuce Wraps:**

Ingredients:

*For the Tuna Salad:*

- 2 cans (5 oz each) canned tuna, drained
- 1/4 cup mayonnaise
- 2 tablespoons Greek yogurt or sour cream
- 1 tablespoon Dijon mustard
- 1 celery stalk, finely chopped
- 1/4 red onion, finely chopped
- 1 tablespoon fresh lemon juice
- Salt and black pepper to taste
- Optional add-ins: chopped pickles, capers, fresh herbs (such as parsley or dill)

*For the Lettuce Wraps:*

- Large lettuce leaves (butter lettuce or iceberg lettuce work well)
- Sliced cucumber, for garnish
- Avocado slices, for garnish
- Cherry tomatoes, halved, for garnish
- Lemon wedges, for serving

Instructions:

    Prepare Tuna Salad:

- In a bowl, combine drained tuna, mayonnaise, Greek yogurt or sour cream, Dijon mustard, chopped celery, chopped red onion, fresh lemon juice, salt, and black pepper. Mix well until all ingredients are thoroughly combined.
- Optionally, add in chopped pickles, capers, or fresh herbs according to your preference.

Assemble Lettuce Wraps:

- Take large lettuce leaves, such as butter lettuce or iceberg lettuce, and lay them flat on a plate or serving platter.

Add Tuna Salad:

- Spoon a generous portion of the tuna salad onto the center of each lettuce leaf.

Garnish:

- Top the tuna salad with sliced cucumber, avocado slices, and halved cherry tomatoes.

Serve:

- Serve the Tuna Salad Lettuce Wraps with lemon wedges on the side.

Enjoy:

- Enjoy these light and flavorful Tuna Salad Lettuce Wraps as a healthy and satisfying meal!

These lettuce wraps are not only delicious but also customizable based on your preferences. You can experiment with different herbs, add-ins, or even spice it up with a pinch of cayenne pepper. They make a great option for a quick lunch, dinner, or even as a snack.

## Vegetarian:

### Lentil and Vegetable Stir-Fry:

Ingredients:

- 1 cup dry lentils (brown or green), rinsed and cooked according to package instructions
- 2 tablespoons vegetable oil
- 1 onion, thinly sliced
- 2 bell peppers, thinly sliced (use a mix of colors for variety)
- 2 carrots, julienned or thinly sliced
- 1 zucchini, sliced
- 1 cup broccoli florets
- 3 cloves garlic, minced
- 1 tablespoon fresh ginger, grated
- 1/4 cup soy sauce
- 1 tablespoon sesame oil
- 1 tablespoon rice vinegar
- 1 tablespoon honey or maple syrup
- 1 tablespoon cornstarch mixed with 2 tablespoons water (optional, for thickening)
- Sesame seeds and chopped green onions for garnish
- Cooked brown rice or quinoa for serving

Instructions:

**Cook Lentils:**
- Rinse and cook lentils according to the package instructions. Set aside.

**Prepare Vegetables:**
- Heat vegetable oil in a large wok or skillet over medium-high heat. Add sliced onions, bell peppers, carrots, zucchini, and broccoli. Stir-fry for 5-7 minutes or until vegetables are tender-crisp.

**Add Garlic and Ginger:**
- Add minced garlic and grated ginger to the vegetables. Stir-fry for an additional 1-2 minutes until fragrant.

**Add Cooked Lentils:**
- Add the cooked lentils to the vegetable mixture. Stir to combine.

**Prepare Sauce:**
- In a small bowl, whisk together soy sauce, sesame oil, rice vinegar, and honey or maple syrup.

**Pour Sauce Over Stir-Fry:**
- Pour the sauce over the lentil and vegetable mixture. Toss everything together until well coated.

**Optional Thickening:**
- If you prefer a thicker sauce, mix 1 tablespoon of cornstarch with 2 tablespoons of water. Add this mixture to the stir-fry and stir until the sauce thickens slightly.

**Garnish and Serve:**
- Garnish the Lentil and Vegetable Stir-Fry with sesame seeds and chopped green onions. Serve over cooked brown rice or quinoa.

**Enjoy:**

- Enjoy this wholesome and flavorful Lentil and Vegetable Stir-Fry as a nutritious and satisfying meal!

Feel free to customize the vegetables based on what you have on hand or your personal preferences. This dish is a great way to incorporate lentils and a variety of colorful vegetables into your diet.

**Stuffed Bell Peppers with Quinoa and Black Beans:**

Ingredients:

- 4 large bell peppers, halved and seeds removed
- 1 cup quinoa, rinsed
- 2 cups vegetable broth or water
- 1 can (15 oz) black beans, drained and rinsed
- 1 cup corn kernels (fresh or frozen)
- 1 cup diced tomatoes
- 1 cup shredded cheese (cheddar, Monterey Jack, or a blend)
- 1 teaspoon ground cumin
- 1 teaspoon chili powder
- 1/2 teaspoon garlic powder
- Salt and black pepper to taste
- Olive oil for drizzling
- Fresh cilantro or parsley for garnish (optional)
- Sour cream or Greek yogurt for serving (optional)

Instructions:

Preheat the Oven:
- Preheat your oven to 375°F (190°C).

Prepare Bell Peppers:
- Cut the bell peppers in half, removing the seeds and membranes. Place them in a baking dish.

Cook Quinoa:

- In a saucepan, combine quinoa and vegetable broth (or water). Bring to a boil, then reduce heat, cover, and simmer for 15-20 minutes or until quinoa is cooked and liquid is absorbed.

Prepare Filling:

- In a large mixing bowl, combine cooked quinoa, black beans, corn, diced tomatoes, shredded cheese, ground cumin, chili powder, garlic powder, salt, and black pepper. Mix well to combine.

Stuff Bell Peppers:

- Spoon the quinoa and black bean mixture into each bell pepper half, pressing down gently to pack the filling.

Drizzle with Olive Oil:

- Drizzle the stuffed bell peppers with a bit of olive oil.

Bake:

- Cover the baking dish with aluminum foil and bake in the preheated oven for 25-30 minutes or until the peppers are tender.

Optional Broil:

- If you'd like a golden top, you can remove the foil and broil the stuffed peppers for an additional 2-3 minutes until the cheese is bubbly and slightly browned.

Garnish and Serve:

- Garnish with fresh cilantro or parsley if desired. Serve the stuffed bell peppers hot.

Optional Toppings:

- Serve with a dollop of sour cream or Greek yogurt on top if you like.

Enjoy:

- Enjoy these Quinoa and Black Bean Stuffed Bell Peppers as a wholesome and satisfying meal!

This recipe is versatile, and you can customize it by adding your favorite herbs, spices, or additional vegetables to the quinoa and black bean mixture. It's a great way to incorporate healthy ingredients into a delicious dish.

**Eggplant and Chickpea Curry:**

Ingredients:

- 1 large eggplant, diced
- 1 can (15 oz) chickpeas, drained and rinsed
- 1 onion, finely chopped
- 3 cloves garlic, minced
- 1 tablespoon fresh ginger, grated
- 1 can (14 oz) diced tomatoes
- 1 can (14 oz) coconut milk
- 2 tablespoons curry powder
- 1 teaspoon ground cumin
- 1 teaspoon ground coriander
- 1/2 teaspoon turmeric
- 1/2 teaspoon cayenne pepper (adjust to taste)
- Salt and black pepper to taste
- 2 tablespoons vegetable oil
- Fresh cilantro for garnish
- Cooked rice or naan for serving

Instructions:

Prepare Ingredients:

- Dice the eggplant, finely chop the onion, mince the garlic, and grate the fresh ginger.

Sauté Onion, Garlic, and Ginger:

- Heat vegetable oil in a large pot or skillet over medium heat. Add chopped onion and sauté until softened. Add minced garlic and grated ginger, sauté for an additional minute until fragrant.

Add Spices:

- Add curry powder, ground cumin, ground coriander, turmeric, cayenne pepper, salt, and black pepper. Stir well to coat the onions, garlic, and ginger with the spices.

Add Eggplant:

- Add the diced eggplant to the pot and stir to coat with the spice mixture. Cook for 5-7 minutes until the eggplant starts to soften.

Add Chickpeas, Tomatoes, and Coconut Milk:

- Add drained and rinsed chickpeas, diced tomatoes (with their juices), and coconut milk to the pot. Stir to combine.

Simmer:

- Bring the mixture to a simmer, then reduce the heat to low. Cover and let it simmer for 20-25 minutes, or until the eggplant is tender and the flavors have melded.

Adjust Seasoning:

- Taste and adjust the seasoning, adding more salt, pepper, or cayenne pepper if needed.

Serve:

- Serve the Eggplant and Chickpea Curry over cooked rice or with naan bread.

Garnish:

- Garnish with fresh cilantro before serving.

Enjoy:

- Enjoy this flavorful and satisfying Eggplant and Chickpea Curry!

This curry is not only delicious but also versatile. Feel free to customize it by adding other vegetables like spinach or bell peppers. Adjust the spice levels according to your preference. It's a comforting and nutritious dish that pairs well with rice or naan for a complete meal.

**Portobello Mushroom Burger:**

Ingredients:

- 4 large Portobello mushrooms, stems removed
- 4 burger buns
- 4 slices of Swiss or your favorite cheese
- 1/4 cup balsamic vinegar
- 2 tablespoons soy sauce
- 2 tablespoons olive oil
- 2 cloves garlic, minced
- 1 teaspoon dried thyme or your favorite herbs
- Salt and black pepper to taste
- Burger toppings (lettuce, tomato, onion, pickles, etc.)
- Condiments of your choice (mayonnaise, mustard, ketchup)

Instructions:

Marinate the Portobello Mushrooms:
- In a bowl, whisk together balsamic vinegar, soy sauce, olive oil, minced garlic, dried thyme, salt, and black pepper.
- Place the Portobello mushrooms in a shallow dish, gill side up. Pour the marinade over the mushrooms, ensuring they are well coated. Let them marinate for at least 30 minutes, turning them occasionally.

Grill or Cook:
- Preheat your grill or a grill pan on medium-high heat. Grill the marinated Portobello mushrooms for about 4-5 minutes on each side, or until they

are tender and have nice grill marks. You can also roast them in the oven at 400°F (200°C) for about 15-20 minutes.

Melt Cheese:

- In the last minute of grilling, place a slice of cheese on each mushroom and close the lid to let it melt.

Toast Buns:

- While the mushrooms are grilling, lightly toast the burger buns on the grill or in a toaster.

Assemble Burgers:

- Place the grilled Portobello mushrooms with melted cheese on the bottom half of each bun.
- Add your favorite burger toppings such as lettuce, tomato, onion, and pickles.

Add Condiments:

- Spread condiments of your choice on the top half of the bun, such as mayonnaise, mustard, or ketchup.

Serve:

- Assemble the burgers, placing the top bun over the toppings.

Enjoy:

- Enjoy your flavorful and satisfying Portobello Mushroom Burger!

These Portobello Mushroom Burgers are a tasty alternative for both vegetarians and meat-lovers alike. The marinated mushrooms add a burst of flavor, and the melted cheese contributes to a satisfyingly savory experience. Feel free to customize your toppings and condiments to suit your preferences.

**Sweet Potato and Black Bean Enchiladas:**

Ingredients:

*For the Filling:*

- 2 medium sweet potatoes, peeled and diced
- 1 can (15 oz) black beans, drained and rinsed
- 1 small red onion, finely chopped
- 1 bell pepper, diced
- 2 cloves garlic, minced
- 1 teaspoon ground cumin
- 1 teaspoon chili powder
- Salt and black pepper to taste
- 2 tablespoons olive oil

*For the Enchilada Sauce:*

- 2 cups tomato sauce or enchilada sauce
- 1 teaspoon ground cumin
- 1 teaspoon chili powder
- Salt to taste

*For Assembly:*

- 8 small flour or corn tortillas
- 2 cups shredded cheese (cheddar, Monterey Jack, or a blend)
- Fresh cilantro, chopped, for garnish

- Sour cream, for serving (optional)
- Sliced avocado, for serving (optional)

Instructions:

Preheat Oven:
- Preheat your oven to 375°F (190°C).

Roast Sweet Potatoes:
- Toss diced sweet potatoes with olive oil, ground cumin, chili powder, salt, and black pepper. Roast in the oven for about 20-25 minutes or until tender.

Prepare Filling:
- In a large bowl, combine the roasted sweet potatoes, black beans, red onion, bell pepper, minced garlic, ground cumin, chili powder, salt, and black pepper. Mix well.

Make Enchilada Sauce:
- In a saucepan, heat tomato sauce or enchilada sauce over medium heat. Add ground cumin, chili powder, and salt. Stir well and let it simmer for a few minutes.

Assemble Enchiladas:
- Spread a small amount of enchilada sauce in the bottom of a baking dish.
- Warm the tortillas according to the package instructions. Spoon a generous portion of the sweet potato and black bean filling onto each tortilla, roll it up, and place it seam-side down in the baking dish.

Pour Sauce and Add Cheese:

- Pour the remaining enchilada sauce over the rolled tortillas. Sprinkle shredded cheese over the top.

Bake:

- Bake in the preheated oven for about 20-25 minutes, or until the cheese is melted and bubbly.

Garnish and Serve:

- Remove from the oven and garnish with chopped cilantro. Serve the Sweet Potato and Black Bean Enchiladas with optional toppings like sour cream and sliced avocado.

Enjoy:

- Enjoy these flavorful and satisfying Sweet Potato and Black Bean Enchiladas!

These enchiladas are a great option for a meatless meal that doesn't compromise on taste. The sweet potatoes add a natural sweetness, and the black beans provide protein and fiber. Customize the recipe with your favorite toppings and enjoy a delicious vegetarian dish.

**Spinach and Feta Stuffed Mushrooms:**

Ingredients:

- 16 large white mushrooms, cleaned and stems removed
- 2 tablespoons olive oil
- 1 small onion, finely chopped
- 2 cloves garlic, minced
- 2 cups fresh spinach, chopped
- 1/2 cup feta cheese, crumbled
- 1/4 cup grated Parmesan cheese
- 1/4 cup breadcrumbs
- Salt and black pepper to taste
- Fresh parsley, chopped, for garnish

Instructions:

Preheat Oven:

- Preheat your oven to 375°F (190°C).

Prepare Mushrooms:

- Clean the mushrooms with a damp cloth and remove the stems. Place the mushroom caps on a baking sheet.

Prepare Filling:

- Chop the mushroom stems finely. In a skillet, heat olive oil over medium heat. Add chopped onion and minced garlic. Sauté until the onion is softened.

Add Spinach:

- Add chopped spinach to the skillet and cook until it wilts.

Combine Ingredients:

- In a bowl, combine the sautéed mixture with crumbled feta cheese, grated Parmesan cheese, breadcrumbs, salt, and black pepper. Mix well.

Stuff Mushrooms:

- Using a spoon, fill each mushroom cap with the spinach and feta mixture, pressing it down slightly.

Bake:

- Bake in the preheated oven for about 15-20 minutes or until the mushrooms are tender and the filling is golden brown.

Garnish:

- Garnish with chopped fresh parsley before serving.

Serve:

- Serve the Spinach and Feta Stuffed Mushrooms warm as a delicious appetizer.

Enjoy:

- Enjoy these flavorful and cheesy stuffed mushrooms!

These Spinach and Feta Stuffed Mushrooms are a crowd-pleaser and perfect for parties or gatherings. The combination of spinach and feta creates a savory and satisfying filling. Adjust the seasonings to your taste and get creative with additional herbs or spices if desired.

**Cauliflower Pizza Crust with Veggie Toppings:**

Ingredients:

*For the Cauliflower Pizza Crust:*

- 1 medium-sized cauliflower head, grated or processed into rice
- 1 cup mozzarella cheese, shredded
- 1 large egg
- 1 teaspoon dried oregano
- 1/2 teaspoon garlic powder
- Salt and black pepper to taste
- Olive oil for greasing

*For the Veggie Toppings:*

- Tomato sauce or pizza sauce
- Mozzarella cheese, shredded
- Bell peppers, thinly sliced
- Cherry tomatoes, halved
- Red onion, thinly sliced
- Mushrooms, sliced
- Fresh basil, chopped, for garnish
- Crushed red pepper flakes (optional)

Instructions:

Preheat Oven:

- Preheat your oven to 425°F (220°C).

Prepare Cauliflower Rice:

- Grate the cauliflower using a box grater or pulse it in a food processor until it resembles rice.

Cook Cauliflower Rice:

- Place the grated cauliflower in a microwave-safe bowl and microwave for about 4-5 minutes, or until it's cooked. Let it cool for a few minutes.

Drain Excess Moisture:

- Place the cooked cauliflower in a clean kitchen towel or cheesecloth. Squeeze out as much moisture as possible. This step is crucial for a crispy crust.

Mix Ingredients:

- In a bowl, combine the drained cauliflower, shredded mozzarella cheese, egg, dried oregano, garlic powder, salt, and black pepper. Mix well until a dough forms.

Shape the Crust:

- Place the cauliflower dough on a parchment-lined baking sheet. With your hands, shape it into a round crust, about 1/4 inch thick.

Bake the Crust:

- Bake the cauliflower crust in the preheated oven for 15-20 minutes or until it's golden brown and firm.

Add Toppings:

- Remove the crust from the oven and spread tomato or pizza sauce evenly over the surface. Add shredded mozzarella cheese and your choice of veggie toppings, such as bell peppers, cherry tomatoes, red onion, and mushrooms.

Bake Again:

- Place the pizza back in the oven and bake for an additional 10-15 minutes, or until the cheese is melted and bubbly.

Garnish and Serve:

- Garnish with fresh basil and optional crushed red pepper flakes. Slice and serve your Cauliflower Pizza with Veggie Toppings.

Enjoy:

- Enjoy a delicious and healthier pizza with a cauliflower crust!

Feel free to get creative with the toppings and customize your cauliflower pizza to suit your preferences. This crust provides a tasty and nutritious alternative for those looking to reduce carb intake or avoid gluten.

**Zucchini and Tomato Gratin:**

Ingredients:

- 3 medium-sized zucchini, thinly sliced
- 4 large tomatoes, thinly sliced
- 1 onion, thinly sliced
- 2 cloves garlic, minced
- 1/2 cup grated Parmesan cheese
- 1/2 cup breadcrumbs
- 1/4 cup fresh basil, chopped
- 2 tablespoons fresh thyme leaves
- Salt and black pepper to taste
- Olive oil for drizzling

Instructions:

Preheat Oven:

- Preheat your oven to 375°F (190°C).

Prepare Vegetables:

- Thinly slice the zucchini, tomatoes, and onion.

Sauté Onion and Garlic:

- In a skillet, heat a bit of olive oil over medium heat. Sauté the sliced onion until softened. Add minced garlic and cook for an additional 1-2 minutes until fragrant.

Assemble Gratin:

- In a baking dish, layer the sliced zucchini, tomatoes, and sautéed onion and garlic, alternating between them. Season each layer with salt and black pepper.

Combine Parmesan and Breadcrumbs:

- In a bowl, mix together grated Parmesan cheese and breadcrumbs.

Top with Parmesan Mixture:

- Sprinkle the Parmesan and breadcrumb mixture over the top layer of tomatoes and zucchini.

Add Fresh Herbs:

- Scatter fresh basil and thyme leaves over the gratin.

Drizzle with Olive Oil:

- Drizzle the top of the gratin with a bit of olive oil.

Bake:

- Bake in the preheated oven for approximately 30-35 minutes or until the vegetables are tender and the top is golden brown.

Garnish and Serve:

- Remove from the oven and let it cool slightly. Garnish with additional fresh herbs if desired.

Enjoy:

- Serve the Zucchini and Tomato Gratin as a delicious side dish or a light vegetarian main course.

This Zucchini and Tomato Gratin is a delightful way to highlight the flavors of seasonal vegetables. It makes for a colorful and tasty addition to your summer meals. Adjust the seasonings and herbs to suit your taste preferences.

**Quinoa and Black Bean Quesadillas:**

Ingredients:

- 1 cup cooked quinoa
- 1 can (15 oz) black beans, drained and rinsed
- 1 cup corn kernels (fresh, frozen, or canned)
- 1 cup diced bell peppers (assorted colors)
- 1 cup shredded cheese (cheddar, Monterey Jack, or a blend)
- 1 teaspoon ground cumin
- 1 teaspoon chili powder
- 1/2 teaspoon garlic powder
- Salt and black pepper to taste
- 8 small flour tortillas
- Olive oil or cooking spray
- Optional toppings: salsa, guacamole, sour cream, chopped cilantro

Instructions:

Prepare Quinoa:
- Cook quinoa according to package instructions. Set aside.

Prepare Filling:
- In a large bowl, combine cooked quinoa, black beans, corn kernels, diced bell peppers, shredded cheese, ground cumin, chili powder, garlic powder, salt, and black pepper. Mix well.

Assemble Quesadillas:

- Place a tortilla on a flat surface. Spoon a portion of the quinoa and black bean mixture onto one-half of the tortilla. Fold the other half over to create a semi-circle.

Cook Quesadillas:

- Heat a large skillet or griddle over medium heat. Lightly brush the surface with olive oil or use cooking spray.
- Place the quesadillas on the skillet and cook for about 2-3 minutes on each side, or until the tortillas are golden brown and the cheese is melted.

Repeat:

- Repeat the process for the remaining quesadillas.

Slice and Serve:

- Remove from the skillet and let them rest for a minute. Slice each quesadilla into wedges.

Optional Toppings:

- Serve with your favorite toppings such as salsa, guacamole, sour cream, and chopped cilantro.

Enjoy:

- Enjoy these Quinoa and Black Bean Quesadillas as a flavorful and satisfying meal!

These quesadillas are not only tasty but also versatile. Feel free to customize them with additional ingredients like diced tomatoes, green onions, or your favorite hot sauce. They make a great lunch or dinner option and are perfect for a quick and easy meal.

**Broccoli and Cheddar Stuffed Potatoes:**

Ingredients:

- 4 large baking potatoes
- 2 cups broccoli florets, steamed or blanched
- 1 cup shredded cheddar cheese
- 1/2 cup sour cream
- 2 tablespoons butter
- Salt and black pepper to taste
- Optional toppings: chopped green onions, crispy bacon bits

Instructions:

Preheat Oven:

- Preheat your oven to 400°F (200°C).

Bake Potatoes:

- Wash the potatoes thoroughly and prick them with a fork. Place them directly on the oven rack and bake for about 45-60 minutes, or until they are tender when pierced with a fork.

Prepare Broccoli:

- While the potatoes are baking, steam or blanch the broccoli until it's just tender. Chop it into small florets.

Cut and Scoop Potatoes:

- Once the potatoes are cooked, let them cool for a few minutes. Cut each potato in half lengthwise. Scoop out the flesh, leaving a thin layer on the skin.

Mash Potatoes:

- In a bowl, mash the scooped-out potato flesh with butter, sour cream, salt, and black pepper. Mix until creamy.

Mix in Broccoli and Cheese:

- Add the chopped broccoli and shredded cheddar cheese to the mashed potatoes. Mix well to combine.

Refill Potato Skins:

- Spoon the mashed potato mixture back into the hollowed-out potato skins.

Bake Again:

- Place the stuffed potatoes on a baking sheet and bake in the preheated oven for an additional 15-20 minutes, or until the cheese is melted and bubbly.

Optional Broil:

- If you'd like a golden-brown top, you can broil the stuffed potatoes for a couple of minutes until the cheese is slightly browned.

Garnish and Serve:

- Remove from the oven and garnish with optional toppings like chopped green onions or crispy bacon bits.

Enjoy:

- Serve these Broccoli and Cheddar Stuffed Potatoes hot and enjoy a comforting and flavorful dish!

These stuffed potatoes are versatile, and you can customize them with additional toppings or spices to suit your taste. They make for a hearty and satisfying meal, perfect for lunch or dinner.

# Chicken Dishes:

**Baked Lemon Garlic Chicken:**

Ingredients:

- 4 boneless, skinless chicken breasts
- 4 cloves garlic, minced
- Zest of 1 lemon
- Juice of 2 lemons
- 2 tablespoons olive oil
- 1 teaspoon dried oregano
- 1 teaspoon dried thyme
- Salt and black pepper to taste
- 1/2 cup chicken broth
- Lemon slices for garnish (optional)
- Fresh parsley, chopped, for garnish

Instructions:

Preheat Oven:
- Preheat your oven to 400°F (200°C).

Prepare Chicken:
- Pat the chicken breasts dry with paper towels and place them in a baking dish.

Make Marinade:

- In a small bowl, whisk together minced garlic, lemon zest, lemon juice, olive oil, dried oregano, dried thyme, salt, and black pepper.

Marinate Chicken:

- Pour the marinade over the chicken breasts, making sure they are well-coated. You can let them marinate for about 15-20 minutes for more flavor, but it's not necessary.

Add Chicken Broth:

- Pour chicken broth into the bottom of the baking dish.

Bake:

- Bake the chicken in the preheated oven for about 25-30 minutes or until the internal temperature reaches 165°F (74°C) and the chicken is cooked through.

Optional Broil:

- If you'd like a golden-brown top, you can broil the chicken for an additional 2-3 minutes until the top is slightly crispy.

Garnish and Serve:

- Remove from the oven, garnish with lemon slices and chopped fresh parsley.

Serve:

- Serve the Baked Lemon Garlic Chicken with your favorite sides, such as roasted vegetables, rice, or a salad.

Enjoy:

- Enjoy this flavorful and juicy Baked Lemon Garlic Chicken!

This dish is not only delicious but also versatile. You can customize the seasoning and herbs to your liking. The combination of lemon and garlic adds a bright and zesty flavor to the chicken.

**Chicken and Vegetable Skewers:**

Ingredients:

- 1.5 lbs (about 700g) boneless, skinless chicken breasts, cut into bite-sized pieces
- 1 bell pepper (red, green, or yellow), cut into chunks
- 1 red onion, cut into chunks
- 1 zucchini, sliced into rounds
- Cherry tomatoes
- 3 tablespoons olive oil
- 2 cloves garlic, minced
- 1 teaspoon dried oregano
- 1 teaspoon dried thyme
- 1 teaspoon smoked paprika
- Salt and black pepper to taste
- Wooden or metal skewers (if using wooden skewers, soak them in water for about 30 minutes before using)

Instructions:

Preheat Grill or Oven:
- Preheat your grill or oven to medium-high heat.

Prepare Marinade:
- In a bowl, whisk together olive oil, minced garlic, dried oregano, dried thyme, smoked paprika, salt, and black pepper.

Marinate Chicken:

- Place the chicken pieces in the marinade, making sure they are well-coated. Let them marinate for at least 15-30 minutes to absorb the flavors.

Assemble Skewers:

- Thread the marinated chicken pieces, bell pepper chunks, red onion chunks, zucchini slices, and cherry tomatoes onto the skewers, alternating between them.

Grill or Oven:

- If using a grill: Grill the skewers for about 10-12 minutes, turning occasionally, or until the chicken is cooked through and has a nice char.
- If using an oven: Place the skewers on a baking sheet and bake in the preheated oven for about 15-20 minutes, turning halfway through.

Check Doneness:

- Ensure the chicken reaches an internal temperature of 165°F (74°C).

Garnish and Serve:

- Remove the skewers from the grill or oven. Garnish with fresh herbs like parsley or cilantro if desired.

Serve:

- Serve the Chicken and Vegetable Skewers with your favorite side dishes, such as rice, quinoa, or a simple salad.

Enjoy:

- Enjoy these flavorful and colorful Chicken and Vegetable Skewers!

These skewers are not only tasty but also a great way to incorporate a variety of vegetables into your meal. Feel free to customize the vegetables and seasoning to suit your preferences.

**Grilled Chicken Caesar Salad:**

Ingredients:

*For the Grilled Chicken:*

- 2 boneless, skinless chicken breasts
- 2 tablespoons olive oil
- 1 teaspoon garlic powder
- 1 teaspoon dried oregano
- Salt and black pepper to taste
- Lemon wedges for serving

*For the Caesar Dressing:*

- 1/2 cup mayonnaise
- 1/4 cup grated Parmesan cheese
- 2 tablespoons Dijon mustard
- 2 cloves garlic, minced
- 2 teaspoons anchovy paste (optional)
- 1 tablespoon Worcestershire sauce
- 1 tablespoon red wine vinegar
- Salt and black pepper to taste

*For the Salad:*

- Romaine lettuce, washed and chopped
- Croutons

- Additional Parmesan cheese for topping

Instructions:

Preheat Grill:
- Preheat your grill to medium-high heat.

Prepare Chicken:
- In a bowl, mix olive oil, garlic powder, dried oregano, salt, and black pepper. Coat the chicken breasts with this mixture.

Grill Chicken:
- Grill the chicken breasts for about 6-8 minutes per side or until they reach an internal temperature of 165°F (74°C). Cooking time may vary based on the thickness of the chicken breasts.

Rest Chicken:
- Remove the chicken from the grill and let it rest for a few minutes. Slice it into thin strips.

Make Caesar Dressing:
- In a bowl, whisk together mayonnaise, grated Parmesan cheese, Dijon mustard, minced garlic, anchovy paste (if using), Worcestershire sauce, red wine vinegar, salt, and black pepper. Adjust the seasoning to taste.

Assemble Salad:
- In a large bowl, toss the chopped Romaine lettuce with the Caesar dressing until evenly coated.

Add Chicken and Croutons:
- Arrange the sliced grilled chicken on top of the salad. Add croutons and toss gently to combine.

Serve:

- Divide the salad onto plates. Top with additional Parmesan cheese and serve with lemon wedges on the side.

Enjoy:

- Enjoy this Grilled Chicken Caesar Salad as a satisfying and flavorful meal!

Feel free to customize the salad by adding cherry tomatoes, extra croutons, or even avocado slices. This recipe provides a delicious twist to the classic Caesar Salad by incorporating grilled chicken for added protein and a smoky flavor.

**Cilantro Lime Chicken with Quinoa:**

Ingredients:

*For the Cilantro Lime Chicken:*

- 4 boneless, skinless chicken breasts
- Zest of 2 limes
- Juice of 2 limes
- 1/4 cup chopped fresh cilantro
- 3 cloves garlic, minced
- 2 tablespoons olive oil
- Salt and black pepper to taste

*For the Quinoa:*

- 1 cup quinoa, rinsed
- 2 cups chicken broth or water
- Salt to taste

*For Garnish:*

- Additional chopped cilantro
- Lime wedges

Instructions:

Marinate Chicken:

- In a bowl, combine lime zest, lime juice, chopped cilantro, minced garlic, olive oil, salt, and black pepper. Mix well. Place the chicken breasts in a resealable plastic bag or shallow dish and pour half of the marinade over them. Let it marinate in the refrigerator for at least 30 minutes.

Prepare Quinoa:

- Rinse the quinoa under cold water. In a saucepan, combine quinoa and chicken broth or water. Add a pinch of salt. Bring to a boil, then reduce the heat to low, cover, and simmer for about 15-20 minutes or until the quinoa is cooked and the liquid is absorbed. Fluff the quinoa with a fork.

Grill Chicken:

- Preheat a grill or grill pan over medium-high heat. Grill the marinated chicken breasts for about 6-8 minutes per side or until they reach an internal temperature of 165°F (74°C) and have grill marks. Cooking time may vary based on the thickness of the chicken breasts.

Rest Chicken:

- Remove the chicken from the grill and let it rest for a few minutes. Slice it into thin strips.

Assemble:

- Serve the sliced Cilantro Lime Chicken over a bed of cooked quinoa.

Garnish:

- Drizzle the remaining cilantro lime marinade over the chicken and quinoa. Garnish with additional chopped cilantro and lime wedges.

Enjoy:

- Enjoy this Cilantro Lime Chicken with Quinoa for a light and flavorful meal!

Feel free to customize this dish by adding your favorite vegetables or serving it with a side salad. The combination of cilantro and lime adds a bright and zesty flavor to the chicken, making it a refreshing and satisfying meal.

**Teriyaki Chicken Stir-Fry:**

Ingredients:

*For the Teriyaki Sauce:*

- 1/4 cup soy sauce
- 2 tablespoons mirin (sweet rice wine)
- 2 tablespoons sake or dry white wine
- 2 tablespoons brown sugar
- 1 tablespoon honey
- 1 teaspoon sesame oil
- 1 teaspoon grated ginger
- 2 cloves garlic, minced
- 1 tablespoon cornstarch mixed with 2 tablespoons water (for thickening)

*For the Stir-Fry:*

- 1.5 lbs (about 700g) boneless, skinless chicken breasts, thinly sliced
- 2 tablespoons vegetable oil
- 1 bell pepper, thinly sliced
- 1 carrot, julienned
- 1 cup broccoli florets
- 1 cup snow peas, ends trimmed
- Cooked white or brown rice for serving
- Sesame seeds and chopped green onions for garnish (optional)

Instructions:

**Prepare Teriyaki Sauce:**

- In a bowl, whisk together soy sauce, mirin, sake, brown sugar, honey, sesame oil, grated ginger, and minced garlic.

**Thicken Sauce:**

- In a small bowl, mix cornstarch with water to create a slurry. Stir the slurry into the teriyaki sauce. Set aside.

**Marinate Chicken:**

- Place the sliced chicken in a bowl and pour a small amount of the teriyaki sauce over it. Allow it to marinate for about 10-15 minutes.

**Stir-Fry Chicken:**

- Heat vegetable oil in a large wok or skillet over medium-high heat. Add the marinated chicken and stir-fry until it's cooked through and has a nice sear.

**Add Vegetables:**

- Add the sliced bell pepper, julienned carrot, broccoli florets, and snow peas to the wok. Stir-fry for an additional 3-5 minutes or until the vegetables are crisp-tender.

**Add Teriyaki Sauce:**

- Pour the remaining teriyaki sauce over the chicken and vegetables. Toss everything together to coat evenly.

**Finish Cooking:**

- Continue to stir-fry for another 2-3 minutes until the sauce thickens and everything is well combined.

**Serve:**

- Serve the Teriyaki Chicken Stir-Fry over cooked rice. Garnish with sesame seeds and chopped green onions if desired.

Enjoy:

- Enjoy this delicious Teriyaki Chicken Stir-Fry as a quick and flavorful meal!

Feel free to customize the vegetables based on your preferences, and you can also add a sprinkle of red pepper flakes for some heat if you like. This recipe offers a perfect balance of savory, sweet, and umami flavors.

**Pesto Chicken with Roasted Vegetables:**

Ingredients:

*For the Pesto:*

- 2 cups fresh basil leaves, packed
- 1/2 cup grated Parmesan cheese
- 1/2 cup pine nuts or walnuts
- 3 cloves garlic, minced
- 1/2 cup extra-virgin olive oil
- Salt and black pepper to taste

*For the Chicken and Vegetables:*

- 4 boneless, skinless chicken breasts
- Salt and black pepper to taste
- 1 pound baby potatoes, halved
- 2 carrots, peeled and sliced
- 1 zucchini, sliced
- 1 red bell pepper, sliced
- 1 tablespoon olive oil
- Additional grated Parmesan for serving (optional)

Instructions:

Preheat Oven:

- Preheat your oven to 400°F (200°C).

**Make Pesto:**

- In a food processor, combine basil, grated Parmesan, pine nuts (or walnuts), and minced garlic. Pulse until finely chopped.
- With the processor running, slowly drizzle in the olive oil until the pesto reaches your desired consistency. Season with salt and black pepper. Set aside.

**Prepare Chicken:**

- Season the chicken breasts with salt and black pepper. Place them in a bowl and coat with a few tablespoons of the prepared pesto. Reserve the remaining pesto for later.

**Roast Vegetables:**

- In a large bowl, toss the halved baby potatoes, sliced carrots, zucchini, and red bell pepper with olive oil. Season with salt and black pepper.
- Spread the vegetables on a baking sheet in a single layer. Roast in the preheated oven for about 25-30 minutes or until the vegetables are tender and slightly golden.

**Grill Chicken:**

- While the vegetables are roasting, grill the pesto-coated chicken breasts on a grill pan or skillet over medium-high heat for about 5-6 minutes per side or until fully cooked.

**Assemble:**

- Once the chicken is cooked and the vegetables are roasted, assemble the dish by placing the grilled chicken on a plate alongside the roasted vegetables.

**Drizzle with Pesto:**

- Drizzle the remaining pesto over the grilled chicken and vegetables.

Optional Garnish:

- Optionally, sprinkle with additional grated Parmesan before serving.

Enjoy:

- Enjoy this delicious Pesto Chicken with Roasted Vegetables as a wholesome and flavorful meal!

This dish is not only tasty but also versatile. You can customize the vegetables based on your preferences, and the vibrant flavors of the pesto add a delicious touch to both the chicken and the roasted vegetables.

**Chicken and Broccoli Casserole:**

Ingredients:

- 3 cups cooked chicken, shredded or diced
- 4 cups fresh broccoli florets
- 1 cup mayonnaise
- 1 cup sour cream
- 1 cup shredded cheddar cheese
- 1 cup shredded mozzarella cheese
- 1/2 cup grated Parmesan cheese
- 2 tablespoons Dijon mustard
- 2 cloves garlic, minced
- Salt and black pepper to taste
- 1 teaspoon onion powder
- 1 teaspoon dried oregano
- 1 teaspoon dried thyme
- 1 cup breadcrumbs
- 2 tablespoons melted butter

Instructions:

Preheat Oven:

- Preheat your oven to 375°F (190°C).

Prepare Casserole Dish:

- Grease a 9x13-inch baking dish.

Cook Broccoli:

- Steam or blanch the broccoli florets until they are slightly tender. You can also use frozen broccoli, thawed and drained.

Make Sauce:

- In a large bowl, mix together mayonnaise, sour cream, shredded cheddar cheese, shredded mozzarella cheese, grated Parmesan cheese, Dijon mustard, minced garlic, salt, black pepper, onion powder, dried oregano, and dried thyme.

Combine Chicken, Broccoli, and Sauce:

- Add the cooked chicken and steamed broccoli to the sauce mixture. Stir until everything is well combined.

Transfer to Baking Dish:

- Transfer the chicken and broccoli mixture to the prepared baking dish, spreading it evenly.

Prepare Topping:

- In a small bowl, mix breadcrumbs with melted butter.

Add Topping:

- Sprinkle the breadcrumb mixture evenly over the chicken and broccoli.

Bake:

- Bake in the preheated oven for about 25-30 minutes or until the casserole is hot and bubbly, and the top is golden brown.

Serve:

- Allow the casserole to cool for a few minutes before serving.

Enjoy:

- Enjoy this comforting Chicken and Broccoli Casserole as a hearty and satisfying meal!

Feel free to customize the recipe by adding other vegetables, such as mushrooms or bell peppers, for additional flavor and nutrition. This casserole is a great option for a family-friendly dinner or potluck.

**Honey Mustard Glazed Chicken Thighs:**

Ingredients:

- 4-6 bone-in, skin-on chicken thighs
- Salt and black pepper to taste
- 2 tablespoons olive oil

For the Honey Mustard Glaze:

- 1/4 cup Dijon mustard
- 2 tablespoons whole grain mustard
- 3 tablespoons honey
- 2 tablespoons soy sauce
- 2 cloves garlic, minced
- 1 teaspoon fresh thyme leaves (optional)

Instructions:

Preheat Oven:
- Preheat your oven to 400°F (200°C).

Season Chicken Thighs:
- Pat the chicken thighs dry with paper towels. Season them with salt and black pepper on both sides.

Sear Chicken Thighs:
- Heat olive oil in an oven-safe skillet over medium-high heat. Place the chicken thighs, skin side down, in the skillet and sear for 3-4 minutes or until the skin is golden brown and crispy.

Prepare Honey Mustard Glaze:

- In a small bowl, whisk together Dijon mustard, whole grain mustard, honey, soy sauce, minced garlic, and fresh thyme leaves.

Glaze Chicken:

- Brush the honey mustard glaze over the seared chicken thighs.

Bake:

- Transfer the skillet to the preheated oven and bake for about 25-30 minutes or until the chicken reaches an internal temperature of 165°F (74°C) and the juices run clear.

Baste:

- Baste the chicken with the pan juices halfway through the baking time and once more before serving.

Serve:

- Remove the skillet from the oven, let the chicken rest for a few minutes, and serve hot.

Garnish (Optional):

- Garnish with additional fresh thyme leaves if desired.

Enjoy:

- Enjoy these Honey Mustard Glazed Chicken Thighs with your favorite side dishes!

These chicken thighs are flavorful and juicy, and the honey mustard glaze adds a delightful sweet and savory kick. Serve them with rice, roasted vegetables, or a fresh salad for a complete and satisfying meal.

**Mediterranean Chicken with Olives and Tomatoes:**

Ingredients:

- 4 boneless, skinless chicken breasts
- Salt and black pepper to taste
- 2 tablespoons olive oil
- 4 cloves garlic, minced
- 1 teaspoon dried oregano
- 1 teaspoon dried thyme
- 1 teaspoon paprika
- 1/2 teaspoon red pepper flakes (optional, for heat)
- 1 cup cherry tomatoes, halved
- 1/2 cup Kalamata olives, pitted and halved
- 1/4 cup sun-dried tomatoes, chopped
- 1/4 cup crumbled feta cheese
- Fresh parsley, chopped, for garnish
- Lemon wedges for serving

Instructions:

Preheat Oven:

- Preheat your oven to 375°F (190°C).

Season Chicken:

- Season the chicken breasts with salt and black pepper on both sides.

Sear Chicken:

- In an oven-safe skillet, heat olive oil over medium-high heat. Sear the chicken breasts for about 3-4 minutes per side, or until golden brown.

Add Aromatics and Spices:

- Add minced garlic, dried oregano, dried thyme, paprika, and red pepper flakes (if using) to the skillet. Stir and cook for about 1 minute until the spices become fragrant.

Add Tomatoes and Olives:

- Add halved cherry tomatoes, Kalamata olives, and sun-dried tomatoes to the skillet. Toss them around to coat in the spices.

Bake:

- Transfer the skillet to the preheated oven and bake for about 20-25 minutes or until the chicken is cooked through.

Check Doneness:

- Ensure that the internal temperature of the chicken reaches 165°F (74°C).

Finish with Feta:

- Sprinkle crumbled feta cheese over the chicken and return the skillet to the oven for an additional 3-5 minutes, or until the cheese is slightly melted.

Garnish:

- Remove from the oven, garnish with fresh chopped parsley, and squeeze lemon wedges over the dish.

Serve:

- Serve the Mediterranean Chicken with Olives and Tomatoes hot, accompanied by your favorite side dishes like rice, couscous, or crusty bread.

Enjoy:

- Enjoy this flavorful and vibrant Mediterranean-inspired dish!

This dish combines the rich flavors of olives, tomatoes, and aromatic herbs to create a satisfying and wholesome meal. The feta cheese adds a creamy and tangy element that complements the Mediterranean flavors beautifully.

**BBQ Chicken Lettuce Wraps:**

Ingredients:

- 1 lb boneless, skinless chicken breasts, cooked and shredded
- 1 cup barbecue sauce (choose your favorite)
- 1 tablespoon olive oil
- 1 small red onion, finely diced
- 1 bell pepper (any color), finely diced
- 2 cloves garlic, minced
- Salt and black pepper to taste
- Iceberg or butter lettuce leaves, for wrapping
- Optional toppings: diced tomatoes, shredded cheese, chopped green onions, sour cream

Instructions:

Cook and Shred Chicken:
- Cook the chicken breasts through your preferred method (grilling, baking, or boiling) until fully cooked. Shred the chicken using two forks.

Sauté Vegetables:
- In a large skillet, heat olive oil over medium heat. Add diced red onion, bell pepper, and minced garlic. Sauté until the vegetables are softened.

Add Shredded Chicken:
- Add the shredded chicken to the skillet with the sautéed vegetables.

Add BBQ Sauce:

- Pour the barbecue sauce over the chicken and vegetables. Stir to coat evenly. Allow it to simmer for a few minutes until everything is heated through.

Season:

- Season with salt and black pepper to taste. Adjust the seasoning according to your preference.

Prepare Lettuce Wraps:

- Wash and separate the leaves of iceberg or butter lettuce to use as wraps.

Assemble:

- Spoon the BBQ chicken mixture into the lettuce leaves.

Optional Toppings:

- Add optional toppings such as diced tomatoes, shredded cheese, chopped green onions, or a dollop of sour cream.

Serve:

- Serve the BBQ Chicken Lettuce Wraps immediately.

Enjoy:

- Enjoy these flavorful and light wraps as a refreshing meal!

These BBQ Chicken Lettuce Wraps are not only delicious but also customizable. Feel free to adjust the level of spiciness in the barbecue sauce or add your favorite toppings to enhance the flavors. They make for a satisfying and healthy alternative to traditional wraps.

## Seafood:

**Baked Cod with Herbs:**

Ingredients:

- 4 cod fillets
- 2 tablespoons olive oil
- 2 tablespoons fresh lemon juice
- 2 cloves garlic, minced
- 1 tablespoon fresh parsley, chopped
- 1 teaspoon fresh thyme leaves
- Salt and black pepper to taste
- Lemon wedges for serving

Instructions:

Preheat Oven:

- Preheat your oven to 400°F (200°C).

Prepare Cod Fillets:

- Pat the cod fillets dry with paper towels and place them in a baking dish.

Mix Herbs and Seasonings:

- In a small bowl, mix together olive oil, fresh lemon juice, minced garlic, chopped parsley, fresh thyme leaves, salt, and black pepper.

Coat Cod Fillets:

- Pour the herb mixture over the cod fillets, ensuring they are well coated on all sides.

Marinate (Optional):

- For enhanced flavor, you can let the cod marinate in the herb mixture for about 15-20 minutes before baking.

Bake:

- Bake the cod in the preheated oven for approximately 15-20 minutes, or until the fish is opaque and flakes easily with a fork.

Broil (Optional):

- If you'd like a golden brown crust on top, you can broil the cod for an additional 2-3 minutes after baking.

Check Doneness:

- Ensure the cod reaches an internal temperature of 145°F (63°C).

Serve:

- Remove from the oven and serve the Baked Cod with Herbs with lemon wedges.

Enjoy:

- Enjoy this light and flavorful Baked Cod with Herbs as a healthy and delicious meal!

Feel free to customize the herb mixture based on your preferences. This recipe provides a simple and elegant way to prepare cod, allowing the natural flavors of the fish to shine with the added freshness of herbs and lemon.

**Shrimp and Vegetable Stir-Fry:**

Ingredients:

- 1 pound (450g) large shrimp, peeled and deveined
- 2 cups broccoli florets
- 1 red bell pepper, sliced
- 1 yellow bell pepper, sliced
- 1 carrot, julienned
- 3 cloves garlic, minced
- 1 tablespoon ginger, minced
- 1/4 cup soy sauce
- 2 tablespoons oyster sauce
- 1 tablespoon sesame oil
- 1 tablespoon cornstarch
- 2 tablespoons vegetable oil (for cooking)
- Sesame seeds and green onions for garnish (optional)
- Cooked rice for serving

Instructions:

In a small bowl, mix together soy sauce, oyster sauce, sesame oil, and cornstarch. Set aside.

Heat 1 tablespoon of vegetable oil in a wok or large skillet over medium-high heat.

Add the shrimp to the hot pan and stir-fry for 2-3 minutes, or until they are pink and opaque. Remove the shrimp from the pan and set aside.

In the same pan, add another tablespoon of vegetable oil. Stir in the minced garlic and ginger and cook for about 30 seconds until fragrant.

Add the broccoli, bell peppers, and julienned carrot to the pan. Stir-fry the vegetables for 3-4 minutes until they are crisp-tender.

Return the cooked shrimp to the pan and pour the sauce over the shrimp and vegetables. Stir everything together until the sauce thickens and coats the shrimp and vegetables evenly.

Serve the shrimp and vegetable stir-fry over cooked rice.

Garnish with sesame seeds and chopped green onions if desired.

Enjoy your delicious shrimp and vegetable stir-fry! Feel free to customize the vegetables or adjust the sauce according to your taste preferences.

**Lemon Garlic Butter Salmon:**

Ingredients:

- 4 salmon fillets
- Salt and black pepper to taste
- 2 tablespoons olive oil
- 4 cloves garlic, minced
- 1/4 cup chicken or vegetable broth
- Juice of 1 lemon
- Zest of 1 lemon
- 2 tablespoons unsalted butter
- Chopped fresh parsley for garnish

Instructions:

Preheat your oven to 375°F (190°C).

Season the salmon fillets with salt and black pepper on both sides.

In an oven-safe skillet, heat olive oil over medium-high heat.

Place the salmon fillets in the skillet, skin-side down if they have skin. Sear for 2-3 minutes until the skin is crispy.

Flip the salmon fillets, and add minced garlic to the skillet. Sauté the garlic for about 1 minute until fragrant.

Pour in the chicken or vegetable broth, lemon juice, and lemon zest. Bring the mixture to a simmer.

Transfer the skillet to the preheated oven and bake for 10-12 minutes, or until the salmon is cooked through and flakes easily with a fork.

Remove the skillet from the oven and add butter to the pan. Swirl the skillet to melt the butter and coat the salmon with the lemony garlic butter sauce.

Garnish the salmon with chopped fresh parsley.

Serve the lemon garlic butter salmon over rice, quinoa, or with your favorite side dishes.

This dish is not only delicious but also quick to prepare, making it a great option for a weeknight dinner. Adjust the seasoning and lemon quantities according to your taste preferences. Enjoy your lemon garlic butter salmon!

**Tuna and Avocado Salad:**

Ingredients:

- 2 cans (about 10 ounces each) canned tuna, drained
- 2 ripe avocados, diced
- 1/2 red onion, finely chopped
- 1 cucumber, diced
- 1 cup cherry tomatoes, halved
- 1/4 cup fresh cilantro or parsley, chopped
- Juice of 1-2 limes
- 2 tablespoons extra-virgin olive oil
- Salt and pepper to taste
- Optional: 1 jalapeño, seeds removed and finely chopped for some heat
- Optional: Mixed salad greens for serving

Instructions:

In a large bowl, combine the drained tuna, diced avocados, chopped red onion, diced cucumber, halved cherry tomatoes, and chopped cilantro or parsley.

In a small bowl, whisk together the lime juice, extra-virgin olive oil, salt, and pepper. Adjust the seasoning to taste.

Pour the dressing over the tuna and avocado mixture. Gently toss everything together until well combined.

If you like some heat, add the finely chopped jalapeño to the salad and mix.

Allow the salad to marinate for a few minutes to let the flavors meld.

Serve the tuna and avocado salad on its own or over a bed of mixed salad greens.

This tuna and avocado salad is not only delicious but also packed with healthy fats and protein. It makes a great light lunch or dinner option. Feel free to customize the ingredients based on your preferences, and enjoy this refreshing and nutritious salad!

**Seared Scallops with Asparagus:**

Ingredients:

- 1 pound fresh scallops, patted dry
- Salt and black pepper to taste
- 2 tablespoons olive oil
- 1 pound asparagus spears, tough ends trimmed
- 2 tablespoons unsalted butter
- 2 cloves garlic, minced
- Zest of 1 lemon
- Juice of 1 lemon
- Fresh parsley, chopped, for garnish (optional)
- Lemon wedges, for serving

Instructions:

Prepare the Scallops:
- Ensure the scallops are dry. Season them with salt and pepper on both sides.
- Heat 1 tablespoon of olive oil in a large skillet over medium-high heat.

Sear the Scallops:
- Once the oil is hot, add the scallops to the skillet, making sure not to overcrowd them.
- Sear the scallops for 1-2 minutes on each side, or until they develop a golden crust. Be careful not to overcook; scallops should be tender and slightly translucent in the center.

Cook the Asparagus:

- In a separate pan, heat the remaining 1 tablespoon of olive oil over medium heat.
- Add trimmed asparagus to the pan and sauté for 3-5 minutes, or until they are crisp-tender. Season with salt and pepper.

Combine and Finish:

- Push the asparagus to the sides of the pan and add butter to the center.
- Once the butter is melted, add minced garlic and lemon zest. Sauté for about 1 minute until the garlic is fragrant.

Serve:

- Arrange the seared scallops on a plate with the asparagus.
- Drizzle the lemon juice over the scallops and asparagus.
- Garnish with fresh parsley if desired.
- Serve with lemon wedges on the side.

This seared scallops with asparagus dish is not only visually appealing but also showcases the natural sweetness of the scallops and the freshness of the asparagus. Enjoy this elegant and delicious meal!

**Grilled Mahi-Mahi with Mango Salsa:**

Grilled Mahi-Mahi:

Ingredients:

- 4 Mahi-Mahi fillets
- 2 tablespoons olive oil
- 2 cloves garlic, minced
- 1 teaspoon paprika
- 1 teaspoon cumin
- Salt and black pepper to taste
- Juice of 1 lime
- Fresh cilantro for garnish (optional)

Instructions:

Marinate the Mahi-Mahi:
- In a bowl, mix together olive oil, minced garlic, paprika, cumin, salt, pepper, and lime juice to create a marinade.
- Coat the Mahi-Mahi fillets with the marinade and let them marinate for at least 30 minutes.

Preheat the Grill:
- Preheat your grill to medium-high heat.

Grill the Mahi-Mahi:
- Place the marinated Mahi-Mahi fillets on the preheated grill.
- Grill for about 3-4 minutes per side, or until the fish is opaque and easily flakes with a fork.

Mango Salsa:

Ingredients:

- 1 ripe mango, peeled and diced
- 1/2 red onion, finely chopped
- 1 red bell pepper, diced
- 1 jalapeño, seeds removed and finely chopped
- Juice of 1 lime
- Fresh cilantro, chopped
- Salt and pepper to taste

Instructions:

Prepare the Mango Salsa:

- In a bowl, combine diced mango, chopped red onion, diced red bell pepper, chopped jalapeño, lime juice, and fresh cilantro.
- Season the salsa with salt and pepper to taste. Mix well.

Serve:

- Place the grilled Mahi-Mahi fillets on a serving plate.
- Spoon the mango salsa over the top of each fillet.
- Garnish with additional cilantro if desired.

This Grilled Mahi-Mahi with Mango Salsa is a vibrant and flavorful dish that combines the mild and flaky fish with the sweet and tangy salsa. It's perfect for a light and refreshing meal. Enjoy!

**Cajun Spiced Tilapia with Quinoa:**

Ingredients:

- 4 tilapia fillets
- 2 tablespoons Cajun seasoning
- 1 teaspoon garlic powder
- 1 teaspoon onion powder
- 1 teaspoon smoked paprika
- 1/2 teaspoon dried thyme
- Salt and black pepper to taste
- 2 tablespoons olive oil
- Lemon wedges for serving

Instructions:

Prepare the Cajun Spice Mix:

- In a small bowl, mix together Cajun seasoning, garlic powder, onion powder, smoked paprika, dried thyme, salt, and black pepper.

Season the Tilapia:

- Pat the tilapia fillets dry with a paper towel.
- Rub the Cajun spice mix evenly over both sides of each fillet, ensuring they are well coated.

Cook the Tilapia:

- Heat olive oil in a skillet over medium-high heat.
- Add the tilapia fillets to the skillet and cook for about 3-4 minutes per side or until the fish is opaque and easily flakes with a fork.

## Quinoa:

Ingredients:

- 1 cup quinoa, rinsed
- 2 cups water or vegetable broth
- Salt to taste

Instructions:

Cook the Quinoa:

- In a medium saucepan, combine quinoa and water or vegetable broth.
- Bring to a boil, then reduce heat to low, cover, and simmer for about 15-20 minutes or until the quinoa is cooked and the liquid is absorbed.
- Fluff the quinoa with a fork and season with salt to taste.

Serve:

Place a serving of Cajun spiced tilapia over a bed of cooked quinoa on each plate.

Garnish with fresh parsley or cilantro.

Serve with lemon wedges on the side for squeezing over the fish.

This Cajun Spiced Tilapia with Quinoa is a flavorful and wholesome dish that combines the bold flavors of Cajun seasoning with the mildness of tilapia and the nuttiness of quinoa. Enjoy your delicious and nutritious meal!

**Crab and Avocado Stuffed Bell Peppers:**

Ingredients:

- 4 large bell peppers, halved and seeds removed
- 1 pound lump crab meat, drained
- 2 ripe avocados, diced
- 1/2 cup red onion, finely chopped
- 1/2 cup celery, finely chopped
- 1/4 cup mayonnaise
- 2 tablespoons fresh lemon juice
- 1 teaspoon Dijon mustard
- 1 teaspoon Old Bay seasoning (or to taste)
- Salt and black pepper to taste
- 1 cup shredded cheese (cheddar or a blend), optional for topping
- Fresh parsley or cilantro for garnish

Instructions:

Preheat the Oven:

- Preheat your oven to 375°F (190°C).

Prepare Bell Peppers:

- Cut the bell peppers in half lengthwise, removing the seeds and membranes.
- Place the pepper halves in a baking dish, cut side up.

Prepare the Filling:

- In a large bowl, combine lump crab meat, diced avocados, chopped red onion, chopped celery, mayonnaise, lemon juice, Dijon mustard, Old Bay seasoning, salt, and black pepper.
- Gently fold the ingredients together until well combined.

Stuff the Peppers:

- Spoon the crab and avocado mixture into each bell pepper half, pressing it down gently.

Optional Cheese Topping:

- If desired, sprinkle shredded cheese over the stuffed peppers.

Bake:

- Bake in the preheated oven for 20-25 minutes or until the peppers are tender and the filling is heated through.

Garnish and Serve:

- Remove from the oven and garnish with fresh parsley or cilantro.
- Serve the crab and avocado stuffed bell peppers warm.

This Crab and Avocado Stuffed Bell Peppers recipe combines the sweetness of crab meat with the creamy texture of avocados, creating a flavorful and satisfying dish. The addition of Old Bay seasoning adds a touch of warmth and spice. Enjoy your delicious stuffed peppers!

**Spicy Sriracha Shrimp Lettuce Wraps:**

Ingredients:

*For the Sriracha Shrimp:*

- 1 pound large shrimp, peeled and deveined
- 3 tablespoons soy sauce
- 2 tablespoons Sriracha sauce (adjust to your spice preference)
- 1 tablespoon honey
- 1 tablespoon sesame oil
- 2 cloves garlic, minced
- 1 teaspoon grated ginger
- 1 tablespoon olive oil (for cooking)
- Green onions, chopped, for garnish

*For the Lettuce Wraps:*

- Large lettuce leaves (such as iceberg or butter lettuce)
- 1 cup julienned carrots
- 1 cup cucumber, thinly sliced
- Fresh cilantro leaves, for garnish
- Lime wedges, for serving

Instructions:

    Prepare the Sriracha Shrimp:

- In a bowl, whisk together soy sauce, Sriracha sauce, honey, sesame oil, minced garlic, and grated ginger.
- Add the peeled and deveined shrimp to the marinade and let it marinate for at least 15-20 minutes.

Cook the Shrimp:

- Heat olive oil in a skillet over medium-high heat.
- Add the marinated shrimp to the skillet and cook for 2-3 minutes on each side or until they are opaque and cooked through.

Assemble the Lettuce Wraps:

- Place a few shrimp in the center of each lettuce leaf.
- Top with julienned carrots, sliced cucumber, and fresh cilantro.

Garnish and Serve:

- Garnish with chopped green onions and serve with lime wedges on the side.

Serve:

- Serve the Spicy Sriracha Shrimp Lettuce Wraps immediately, allowing everyone to customize their wraps with additional toppings and lime juice.

These Spicy Sriracha Shrimp Lettuce Wraps are not only packed with flavor but also make for a refreshing and low-carb meal. Adjust the level of Sriracha to suit your spice preference. Enjoy the vibrant combination of spicy shrimp and crisp vegetables!

**Baked Halibut with Roasted Vegetables:**

Ingredients:

*For the Baked Halibut:*

- 4 halibut fillets (about 6 ounces each)
- Salt and black pepper to taste
- 2 tablespoons olive oil
- 2 tablespoons lemon juice
- 2 cloves garlic, minced
- 1 teaspoon dried oregano
- 1 teaspoon dried thyme
- 1 teaspoon paprika
- Lemon wedges for serving

*For the Roasted Vegetables:*

- 2 cups cherry tomatoes, halved
- 2 bell peppers (assorted colors), sliced
- 1 red onion, sliced
- 1 zucchini, sliced
- 2 tablespoons olive oil
- Salt and black pepper to taste
- 1 teaspoon dried Italian seasoning (optional)

Instructions:

Preheat the Oven:

- Preheat your oven to 400°F (200°C).

Prepare the Halibut:

- Pat the halibut fillets dry with a paper towel.
- Place the fillets in a baking dish. Season both sides with salt and black pepper.

Make the Marinade:

- In a small bowl, whisk together olive oil, lemon juice, minced garlic, dried oregano, dried thyme, and paprika.

Marinate the Halibut:

- Pour the marinade over the halibut fillets, ensuring they are well coated. Let them marinate for about 15 minutes.

Prepare the Roasted Vegetables:

- In a large bowl, toss the cherry tomatoes, bell peppers, red onion, and zucchini with olive oil. Season with salt, black pepper, and Italian seasoning if using.

Roast in the Oven:

- Spread the vegetables on a baking sheet in a single layer.
- Place both the marinated halibut and the baking sheet with vegetables in the preheated oven.

Bake:

- Bake for about 15-20 minutes or until the halibut is cooked through, and the vegetables are tender and slightly caramelized.

Serve:

- Serve the baked halibut over a bed of roasted vegetables.
- Garnish with fresh herbs, if desired.

- Serve with lemon wedges on the side.

This Baked Halibut with Roasted Vegetables is a wholesome and well-balanced dish. The lemon and herb-infused halibut pairs perfectly with the flavorful roasted vegetables. It's a simple yet impressive meal for any occasion. Enjoy!

## Desserts:

**Greek Yogurt Parfait with Fresh Fruit:**

Ingredients:

- 2 cups Greek yogurt (plain or vanilla-flavored)
- 2 tablespoons honey or maple syrup (optional, for sweetness)
- 1 cup granola
- 1 cup fresh berries (such as strawberries, blueberries, raspberries)
- 1 banana, sliced
- 1/4 cup chopped nuts (such as almonds or walnuts)
- 1 tablespoon chia seeds (optional)
- Fresh mint leaves for garnish (optional)

Instructions:

Prepare Greek Yogurt:
- In a bowl, mix the Greek yogurt with honey or maple syrup if you want to add sweetness. Adjust the sweetness according to your preference.

Assemble the Parfait:
- In serving glasses or bowls, layer the Greek yogurt with granola, fresh berries, banana slices, chopped nuts, and chia seeds if using.

Repeat Layers:
- Repeat the layers until the glasses are filled or until you've used all the ingredients.

Garnish:

- Garnish the top with additional fresh berries, a drizzle of honey or maple syrup, and mint leaves if desired.

Serve:

- Serve the Greek Yogurt Parfait immediately and enjoy this nutritious and satisfying treat.

Variations:

- You can customize your parfait by adding other fruits like sliced peaches, kiwi, or mango.
- Experiment with different types of granola, including nut-free or gluten-free options.
- Consider adding a dollop of nut butter or a sprinkle of coconut flakes for extra flavor.

This Greek Yogurt Parfait with Fresh Fruit is not only delicious but also packed with protein, fiber, and various nutrients. It's a versatile recipe that you can adapt based on your preferences and the fruits available. Enjoy this refreshing and nutritious parfait!

**Dark Chocolate-Dipped Strawberries:**

Ingredients:

- Fresh strawberries, washed and dried
- 6 ounces (about 170g) dark chocolate (at least 70% cocoa), chopped
- 1 teaspoon coconut oil or vegetable oil (optional, for smoother chocolate)
- Toppings (optional):
    - Chopped nuts (e.g., almonds, pistachios)
    - Shredded coconut
    - Sprinkles
    - Sea salt

Instructions:

Prepare a Baking Sheet:
- Line a baking sheet with parchment paper. This will prevent the chocolate-dipped strawberries from sticking.

Melt the Dark Chocolate:
- Place the chopped dark chocolate in a heatproof bowl.
- If desired, add coconut oil to the chocolate. This helps create a smoother consistency.
- Melt the chocolate using a double boiler or by microwaving in 20-30 second intervals, stirring well after each interval until smooth.

Dip the Strawberries:
- Hold each strawberry by the stem and dip it into the melted chocolate, covering about two-thirds of the strawberry.

Let Excess Chocolate Drip:
- Allow any excess chocolate to drip off back into the bowl.

Optional Toppings:
- If using toppings, sprinkle them over the chocolate-dipped part of the strawberry while the chocolate is still wet.

Place on Parchment Paper:
- Place the dipped strawberries on the prepared baking sheet.

Let Chocolate Set:
- Allow the chocolate to set by placing the baking sheet in the refrigerator for about 15-20 minutes.

Serve:
- Once the chocolate is fully set, transfer the dark chocolate-dipped strawberries to a serving plate.

Enjoy:
- Enjoy these delicious treats as a snack or dessert.

Tips:

- Make sure the strawberries are completely dry before dipping them in chocolate to help the chocolate adhere better.
- Feel free to experiment with different types of dark chocolate and toppings to suit your taste preferences.

These Dark Chocolate-Dipped Strawberries are perfect for special occasions, celebrations, or simply as a sweet and satisfying treat. They also make a lovely addition to dessert platters. Enjoy!

**Baked Apple with Cinnamon and Nutmeg:**

Ingredients:

- 4 medium-sized apples (such as Granny Smith or Honeycrisp)
- 2 tablespoons unsalted butter, melted
- 2 tablespoons brown sugar
- 1 teaspoon ground cinnamon
- 1/2 teaspoon ground nutmeg
- 1/4 cup chopped nuts (such as walnuts or pecans), optional
- Vanilla ice cream or whipped cream for serving, optional

Instructions:

Preheat the Oven:

- Preheat your oven to 375°F (190°C).

Prepare the Apples:

- Wash and core the apples. You can leave the skin on for added texture and nutrients.

Mix the Filling:

- In a small bowl, mix together melted butter, brown sugar, ground cinnamon, and ground nutmeg.

Fill the Apples:

- Place the cored apples in a baking dish.
- Spoon the butter and spice mixture evenly into the center of each apple.

Optional Nuts:

- If using nuts, sprinkle them over the top of each apple.

Bake:

- Bake in the preheated oven for about 25-30 minutes, or until the apples are tender. The baking time may vary depending on the size and type of apples.

Serve:

- Remove the baked apples from the oven and let them cool slightly.
- Serve the baked apples warm, optionally with a scoop of vanilla ice cream or a dollop of whipped cream.

Enjoy:

- Enjoy the warm and fragrant baked apples with the comforting flavors of cinnamon and nutmeg.

This simple Baked Apple with Cinnamon and Nutmeg recipe is a delightful way to enjoy the natural sweetness of apples with warm, aromatic spices. It's a perfect dessert for a cozy evening or a comforting treat during the fall season.

**Berry Sorbet with Mint:**

Ingredients:

- 3 cups mixed berries (such as strawberries, blueberries, raspberries)
- 1/2 cup granulated sugar (adjust based on your sweetness preference)
- 1 tablespoon fresh lime or lemon juice
- 1/4 cup fresh mint leaves, plus extra for garnish
- 1 cup cold water
- Mint sprigs for garnish (optional)

Instructions:

Prepare the Berries:

- Wash the berries thoroughly and remove any stems. If using strawberries, hull and slice them.

Make the Simple Syrup:

- In a small saucepan, combine sugar and cold water. Heat over medium heat, stirring until the sugar dissolves. Allow it to cool.

Blend the Ingredients:

- In a blender, combine the mixed berries, fresh lime or lemon juice, mint leaves, and the cooled simple syrup. Blend until smooth.

Strain the Mixture:

- If you prefer a smoother sorbet, strain the mixture through a fine-mesh sieve to remove seeds and pulp. Press down with a spoon to extract as much liquid as possible.

Chill the Mixture:

- Transfer the blended mixture to a bowl and refrigerate for at least 2-3 hours or until well chilled.

Churn in an Ice Cream Maker:

- If you have an ice cream maker, follow the manufacturer's instructions for churning the sorbet. This step typically takes 20-30 minutes.

Freeze Without an Ice Cream Maker:

- If you don't have an ice cream maker, pour the chilled mixture into a shallow dish. Place it in the freezer and stir every 30 minutes with a fork to break up ice crystals until the sorbet reaches the desired consistency.

Serve:

- Scoop the berry sorbet into serving bowls or glasses.
- Garnish with fresh mint leaves and mint sprigs if desired.

Enjoy:

- Enjoy this refreshing and fruity berry sorbet with the delightful hint of mint.

This Berry Sorbet with Mint is not only delicious but also a healthier alternative to store-bought desserts. It's a delightful way to enjoy the natural sweetness of berries with a burst of minty freshness.

**Avocado Chocolate Mousse:**

Ingredients:

- 2 ripe avocados, peeled and pitted
- 1/2 cup cocoa powder
- 1/2 cup maple syrup or honey (adjust to taste)
- 1/4 cup almond milk or any milk of your choice
- 1 teaspoon vanilla extract
- A pinch of salt
- Optional toppings: whipped cream, berries, chopped nuts, or grated chocolate

Instructions:

Blend Avocados:

- In a blender or food processor, combine the ripe avocados, cocoa powder, maple syrup or honey, almond milk, vanilla extract, and a pinch of salt.

Blend Until Smooth:

- Blend the ingredients until smooth and creamy. Scrape down the sides of the blender or processor as needed to ensure everything is well combined.

Adjust Sweetness:

- Taste the chocolate mousse and adjust the sweetness if needed by adding more maple syrup or honey.

Chill:

- Transfer the chocolate mousse to a bowl or individual serving glasses.
- Cover and refrigerate for at least 2 hours to allow the mousse to chill and firm up.

Serve:

- Once chilled, you can serve the avocado chocolate mousse as is or with your favorite toppings.

Optional Toppings:

- Top with whipped cream, fresh berries, chopped nuts, or grated chocolate for extra flavor and texture.

Enjoy:

- Enjoy this creamy and delicious avocado chocolate mousse guilt-free!

This Avocado Chocolate Mousse is a healthier alternative to traditional chocolate mousse, as avocados provide a rich and creamy texture while also offering numerous nutritional benefits. It's a great way to satisfy your chocolate cravings while incorporating the goodness of avocados into your dessert.

**Chia Seed Pudding with Berries:**

Ingredients:

- 1/4 cup chia seeds
- 1 cup milk (dairy or plant-based like almond, coconut, or soy)
- 1-2 tablespoons maple syrup or honey (adjust to taste)
- 1/2 teaspoon vanilla extract
- Mixed berries (strawberries, blueberries, raspberries) for topping
- Optional toppings: sliced almonds, shredded coconut, or a drizzle of honey

Instructions:

Mix Chia Seeds and Liquid:

- In a bowl, combine chia seeds, milk, maple syrup or honey, and vanilla extract. Whisk well to ensure the chia seeds are evenly distributed.

Let It Set:

- Cover the bowl and refrigerate for at least 4 hours or, ideally, overnight. This allows the chia seeds to absorb the liquid and create a pudding-like consistency.

Stir Before Serving:

- After the chia pudding has set, give it a good stir to break up any clumps and achieve a smooth texture.

Assemble Pudding Cups:

- Spoon the chia pudding into serving cups or jars.

Add Berries:

- Top the chia pudding with a generous amount of mixed berries.

Optional Toppings:

- If desired, add additional toppings such as sliced almonds, shredded coconut, or a drizzle of honey for extra flavor and texture.

Serve:

- Serve the chia seed pudding with berries immediately or refrigerate until ready to eat.

Enjoy:

- Enjoy this nutritious and satisfying chia seed pudding with the burst of freshness from the mixed berries.

Chia seed pudding is not only tasty but also packed with fiber, omega-3 fatty acids, and various nutrients. Customize it with your favorite berries and toppings for a delightful and wholesome treat. This recipe is versatile, so feel free to experiment with different flavors and textures based on your preferences.

**Frozen Banana Bites with Almond Butter:**

Ingredients:

- 2 large bananas, peeled and sliced into rounds
- Almond butter (or any nut butter of your choice)
- Dark chocolate, melted (optional)
- Chopped nuts (such as almonds or peanuts), shredded coconut, or chia seeds for coating (optional)

Instructions:

Prepare Banana Slices:

- Slice the bananas into rounds, about 1/2-inch thick.

Assemble Banana Bites:

- Take one banana slice and spread a small amount of almond butter on top.
- Place another banana slice on top, creating a banana "sandwich" with almond butter in the middle.

Optional Chocolate Coating:

- If desired, you can dip the banana bites in melted dark chocolate. To do this, melt the dark chocolate in a microwave-safe bowl in 20-30 second intervals, stirring in between until smooth.

Coat with Toppings:

- After dipping in chocolate, you can roll the banana bites in chopped nuts, shredded coconut, or chia seeds for added texture and flavor.

Freeze:

- Place the assembled banana bites on a parchment-lined tray or plate.
- Freeze for at least 2-3 hours or until the banana bites are firm.

Serve:

- Once frozen, the banana bites are ready to be enjoyed. Serve them as a refreshing snack or dessert.

Store:

- If you have any leftovers, store the frozen banana bites in an airtight container in the freezer.

Enjoy:

- Enjoy these delicious frozen banana bites with almond butter whenever you need a sweet and satisfying treat.

This frozen banana bites recipe is not only tasty but also a healthier alternative to traditional frozen desserts. The combination of frozen banana and creamy almond butter creates a delightful texture, while the optional chocolate coating and toppings add extra indulgence. Feel free to get creative with your choice of toppings and coatings.

**Coconut and Mango Rice Pudding:**

Ingredients:

- 1 cup Arborio rice (or any short-grain rice)
- 1 can (13.5 oz) coconut milk
- 2 cups whole milk
- 1/2 cup sugar (adjust to taste)
- 1 teaspoon vanilla extract
- 1/2 cup sweetened shredded coconut
- 1 ripe mango, peeled, pitted, and diced
- Pinch of salt
- Mint leaves for garnish (optional)

Instructions:

Cook the Rice:

- In a medium-sized saucepan, combine the Arborio rice, coconut milk, whole milk, sugar, and a pinch of salt.
- Bring the mixture to a gentle boil, then reduce the heat to low and simmer. Stir occasionally to prevent the rice from sticking to the bottom.

Simmer Until Creamy:

- Simmer the rice mixture uncovered for about 25-30 minutes or until the rice is cooked, and the mixture becomes creamy. Stir regularly.

Add Coconut and Vanilla:

- Stir in the sweetened shredded coconut and vanilla extract during the last 5 minutes of cooking.

Cool the Pudding:

- Once the rice pudding has reached the desired consistency, remove it from the heat and let it cool slightly.

Assemble with Mango:

- Spoon the coconut and mango rice pudding into serving bowls or glasses.
- Top each serving with diced mango.

Chill:

- Refrigerate the rice pudding for at least 2 hours or until it's well chilled.

Garnish and Serve:

- Before serving, garnish with mint leaves if desired.

Enjoy:

- Enjoy this tropical and creamy coconut and mango rice pudding as a refreshing dessert.

This coconut and mango rice pudding is a delicious combination of creamy coconut, sweet mango, and perfectly cooked rice. It's a delightful dessert that brings a taste of the tropics to your table. Feel free to adjust the sweetness and texture according to your preferences.

**Pumpkin Spice Energy Bites:**

Ingredients:

- 1 cup old-fashioned oats
- 1/2 cup pumpkin puree
- 1/4 cup honey or maple syrup
- 1/2 cup almond butter or peanut butter
- 1/2 cup ground flaxseed
- 1 teaspoon pumpkin spice mix (or a combination of cinnamon, nutmeg, ginger, and cloves)
- 1/2 cup chopped nuts (such as walnuts or pecans)
- 1/2 cup shredded coconut (optional, for rolling)
- A pinch of salt

Instructions:

Combine Ingredients:
- In a large bowl, combine old-fashioned oats, pumpkin puree, honey or maple syrup, almond butter or peanut butter, ground flaxseed, pumpkin spice mix, chopped nuts, and a pinch of salt.

Mix Well:
- Stir the ingredients together until well combined. If the mixture seems too wet, you can add a bit more oats. If it's too dry, add a bit more pumpkin puree or nut butter.

Chill:

- Place the mixture in the refrigerator for about 15-30 minutes to make it easier to handle.

Form into Bites:

- Once chilled, take small portions of the mixture and roll them into bite-sized balls using your hands.

Optional Coating:

- If desired, roll the energy bites in shredded coconut for an extra layer of flavor.

Chill Again:

- Place the pumpkin spice energy bites in the refrigerator for another 30 minutes to set.

Store:

- Store the energy bites in an airtight container in the refrigerator for up to a week.

Enjoy:

- Enjoy these tasty pumpkin spice energy bites whenever you need a quick and nutritious snack.

These pumpkin spice energy bites are not only delicious but also packed with fiber, healthy fats, and natural sweetness. They're a perfect snack to satisfy your pumpkin spice cravings while providing a boost of energy. Adjust the sweetness and spice levels according to your taste preferences.

**Yogurt and Berry Popsicles:**

Ingredients:

- 1 cup Greek yogurt (plain or vanilla-flavored)
- 1 cup mixed berries (such as strawberries, blueberries, raspberries)
- 2 tablespoons honey or maple syrup (adjust to taste)
- 1 teaspoon vanilla extract (if using plain yogurt)
- Popsicle molds and sticks

Instructions:

Prepare the Yogurt Mixture:
- In a bowl, mix the Greek yogurt with honey or maple syrup. If you're using plain yogurt, add vanilla extract as well. Stir until well combined.

Blend the Berries:
- In a blender or food processor, blend the mixed berries until you achieve a smooth puree.

Layering in Popsicle Molds:
- Spoon a small amount of the yogurt mixture into each popsicle mold, filling them about one-third full.
- Add a layer of the berry puree on top of the yogurt layer, filling the molds to about two-thirds full.
- Add another layer of the yogurt mixture on top of the berry layer to fill the molds.

Swirl the Layers:

- Use a popsicle stick or a skewer to gently swirl the layers in each mold for a marbled effect.

Insert Popsicle Sticks:

- Place popsicle sticks into each mold, ensuring they are centered.

Freeze:

- Freeze the popsicles for at least 4-6 hours or until they are completely frozen.

Unmold and Enjoy:

- Once frozen, remove the popsicles from the molds by running them under warm water for a few seconds.
- Enjoy your homemade yogurt and berry popsicles!

These yogurt and berry popsicles are not only delicious but also packed with the goodness of yogurt and fresh berries. They make for a perfect guilt-free summer treat that you can customize with your favorite berries and yogurt flavors. Enjoy!

## Beverages:

**Green Tea with Lemon and Mint:**

Ingredients:

- 1 green tea bag or 1 teaspoon loose green tea leaves
- 1 cup hot water (not boiling)
- Fresh mint leaves
- 1/2 lemon, sliced
- Honey or sweetener of choice (optional)

Instructions:

Brew Green Tea:

- Place the green tea bag or loose green tea leaves in a teapot or mug.
- Pour hot water over the tea leaves. Be cautious not to use boiling water as it can make the tea bitter. Allow it to steep for 2-3 minutes.

Add Fresh Mint:

- While the tea is steeping, add a few fresh mint leaves to the teapot or mug. The mint will infuse its aromatic flavor into the tea.

Sweeten (Optional):

- If desired, add honey or your preferred sweetener to the tea. Stir well to dissolve.

Add Lemon Slices:

- After the tea has steeped, add slices of fresh lemon to the teapot or mug. The lemon adds a citrusy zing to the tea.

Strain (If Using Loose Tea):

- If you used loose green tea leaves, strain the tea before serving to remove the leaves.

Serve:

- Pour the green tea with lemon and mint into cups or glasses.

Garnish (Optional):

- Garnish with additional fresh mint leaves or a lemon slice if desired.

Enjoy:

- Sip and enjoy the refreshing and soothing flavor of green tea with lemon and mint.

Green tea with lemon and mint not only tastes great but also offers potential health benefits, as green tea is rich in antioxidants. This beverage is perfect for a relaxing moment or as a pick-me-up during the day. Adjust the sweetness and intensity of the ingredients based on your personal preference.

**Infused Water with Cucumber and Berries:**

Ingredients:

- 1/2 cucumber, thinly sliced
- 1/2 cup mixed berries (such as strawberries, blueberries, raspberries)
- 1-2 sprigs of fresh mint
- Ice cubes
- Water

Instructions:

Prepare Ingredients:
- Wash the cucumber, berries, and mint thoroughly.

Slice Cucumber:
- Cut the cucumber into thin slices. You can also use a vegetable peeler to create cucumber ribbons.

Combine Ingredients in a Pitcher:
- In a large pitcher, combine the cucumber slices, mixed berries, and fresh mint.

Muddle (Optional):
- If you want to intensify the flavor, gently muddle the ingredients with a muddler or the back of a spoon. This helps release the juices and flavors.

Add Ice Cubes:
- Drop a handful of ice cubes into the pitcher. This will keep the infused water cold.

Fill with Water:

- Fill the pitcher with water. Use filtered water for the best taste.

Stir:

- Give the infused water a gentle stir to distribute the flavors.

Refrigerate:

- Place the pitcher in the refrigerator and let it chill for at least 1-2 hours to allow the flavors to infuse.

Serve:

- Pour the infused water into glasses, making sure to include some of the cucumber slices, berries, and mint.

Enjoy:

- Enjoy the crisp and refreshing taste of cucumber and berries infused water.

This infused water is a tasty and healthy alternative to sugary drinks. The combination of cucumber, berries, and mint adds a burst of flavor to your water, making it more enjoyable and appealing. Feel free to experiment with different berries and herbs for variations in flavor.

**Matcha Latte with Almond Milk:**

Ingredients:

- 1 teaspoon Matcha powder
- 1-2 teaspoons sweetener of choice (such as honey, agave syrup, or maple syrup)
- 1 cup almond milk (unsweetened)
- Hot water (about 2 ounces)

Instructions:

Sift Matcha Powder:

- Sift the Matcha powder into a bowl to ensure there are no clumps.

Whisk Matcha:

- Add about 2 ounces of hot water to the Matcha powder. Using a bamboo whisk (chasen) or a small regular whisk, vigorously whisk the Matcha and water in a "W" or "M" motion until it becomes frothy.

Heat Almond Milk:

- In a separate saucepan, heat the almond milk until it is warm but not boiling. You can also heat the almond milk in the microwave.

Sweeten Matcha:

- Add the sweetener of your choice to the Matcha and water mixture. Adjust the sweetness according to your taste.

Combine Matcha and Almond Milk:

- Pour the frothy Matcha mixture into a cup.
- Pour the warm almond milk over the Matcha. Use a spoon to hold back the foam, allowing the liquid to pour first, and then spoon the foam on top.

Stir and Enjoy:

- Give the Matcha Latte a gentle stir to combine the Matcha with the almond milk.

Optional:

- You can sprinkle a little Matcha powder on top for garnish if desired.

Enjoy:

- Sip and savor your delicious Matcha Latte with almond milk!

This Matcha Latte is not only rich in antioxidants but also has a delightful balance of earthy Matcha flavor and the creamy texture of almond milk. Adjust the sweetness and Matcha powder amount to suit your taste preferences. It's a great way to enjoy the benefits of Matcha in a comforting and delicious beverage.

**Berry Smoothie with Spinach:**

Ingredients:

- 1 cup mixed berries (strawberries, blueberries, raspberries)
- 1 ripe banana
- 1 cup fresh spinach leaves, washed
- 1/2 cup Greek yogurt (plain or flavored)
- 1/2 cup almond milk (or any milk of your choice)
- 1 tablespoon chia seeds (optional)
- Ice cubes (optional)
- Honey or maple syrup for sweetness (optional)

Instructions:

Prepare Ingredients:

- Wash the berries and spinach thoroughly. Peel the banana.

Blend:

- In a blender, combine the mixed berries, banana, fresh spinach, Greek yogurt, almond milk, and chia seeds.

Optional Sweetener:

- If you prefer a sweeter smoothie, you can add honey or maple syrup to taste.

Blend Until Smooth:

- Blend all the ingredients until smooth and creamy. If the consistency is too thick, you can add more almond milk to reach your desired thickness.

Add Ice Cubes:

- If you want a colder smoothie, add a handful of ice cubes and blend again until smooth.

Serve:

- Pour the berry smoothie into glasses.

Optional Garnish:

- Garnish with a few whole berries or a sprinkle of chia seeds if desired.

Enjoy:

- Enjoy your refreshing and nutrient-packed Berry Smoothie with Spinach!

This smoothie combines the sweetness of berries and banana with the nutritional boost from fresh spinach, creating a vibrant and flavorful drink. It's an excellent way to start your day or to refuel after a workout. Feel free to customize the recipe by adding other fruits, adjusting sweetness, or incorporating protein powder for an extra protein boost.

**Iced Herbal Tea with Citrus Slices:**

Ingredients:

- 4-5 herbal tea bags (such as peppermint, chamomile, hibiscus, or your favorite herbal blend)
- 4 cups hot water
- 1-2 tablespoons honey or sweetener of choice (optional)
- Ice cubes
- Citrus slices (lemon, lime, orange) for garnish
- Fresh mint leaves for garnish (optional)

Instructions:

Brew Herbal Tea:
- Place the herbal tea bags in a heatproof pitcher.
- Pour hot water over the tea bags. Let the tea steep for about 5-7 minutes or according to the recommended steeping time for the specific herbal tea you're using.

Sweeten (Optional):
- Add honey or sweetener of your choice to the hot tea and stir until dissolved. Adjust the sweetness to your liking.

Cool the Tea:
- Allow the tea to cool to room temperature. You can speed up the process by placing the pitcher in the refrigerator.

Refrigerate:

- Once the tea has cooled, refrigerate it for at least 1-2 hours or until it is well chilled.

Serve Over Ice:

- Fill glasses with ice cubes.
- Pour the chilled herbal tea over the ice.

Garnish with Citrus Slices:

- Add slices of lemon, lime, or orange to the iced tea for a burst of citrus flavor.

Optional Mint Garnish:

- Garnish with fresh mint leaves if desired.

Stir and Enjoy:

- Give the iced herbal tea a gentle stir, and enjoy the refreshing and cooling beverage.

This iced herbal tea with citrus slices is a wonderful way to stay hydrated while enjoying the natural flavors of herbs and citrus. Feel free to experiment with different herbal tea blends and citrus fruits to create your favorite combination. It's a versatile recipe that you can customize based on your taste preferences.